1980

University of St. Francis
GEN   842.9 R665tk
Robl/Æes, Emmanuel.
Three plays /

W9-AOH-019

Southern
Illinois
University
Press

THREE PLAYS BY

Emmanuel Roblès

Plaidoyer pour un rebelle (Case for a Rebel),

L'Horloge (The Clock), and Porfirio

Translated, with an Introduction by James A. Kilker

Foreword by Emmanuel Roblès

With a Bibliography of the Theatre of Roblès
by Marie J. Kilker

Southern Illinois University Press

Carbondale and Edwardsville

Feffer & Simons, Inc.   London and Amsterdam

LIBRARY
College of St. Francis
JOLIET, ILL.

"L'Horloge" suivi de "Porfirio" par Emmanuel Roblès © Édition du Seuil,
1958; *"Plaidoyer pour un rebelle" par Emmanuel Roblès ("Plaidoyer pour un
rebelle" suivi de "Mere Libre")* © Éditions du Seuil, 1965

English translations by James A. Kilker: *Plaidoyer pour un rebelle (Case for
a Rebel)*, copyright © 1973 by James A. Kilker and M. J. Kilker, copyright ©
1977 by Southern Illinois University Press; *L'Horloge (The Clock)*, copyright
© 1972 by Éditions du Seuil, copyright © 1977 by Southern Illinois University
Press; *Porfirio*, copyright © 1972 by Éditions du Seuil, copyright © 1977 by
Southern Illinois University Press

LIBRARY OF CONGRESS CATALOGING IN PUBLICATION DATA

Roblès, Emmanuel.
  Three plays.

  In English.
  CONTENTS: Plaidoyer pour un rebelle (Case for a rebel).—L'horloge (The
clock).—Porfirio.
  PQ2635.01845A25   842'.9'12   77-24662
  ISBN 0-8093-0822-3

Printed in the United States of America
Designed by David Ford

Caution. Professionals and amateurs are hereby warned that *Plaidoyer pour un
rebelle (Case for a Rebel)*, L'Horloge *(The Clock)*, and *Porfirio*, being fully protected under the copyright law of the United States of America, the British
Empire, including the Dominion of Canada, and other countries of the
copyright union, are subject to royalties; and anyone presenting these plays
without the consent of Southern Illinois University Press will be liable to the
penalties by law provided. All applications for the right of amateur or professional productions must be made to the Director, Southern Illinois University
Press, Post Office Box 3697, Carbondale, Illinois 62901.

842.9
R665th

Contents

88983

List of Illustrations

Foreword

BY EMMANUEL ROBLÈS OF THE GONCOURT ACADEMY

The choice of these three plays is due to my friend and translator James A. Kilker who has singled out a tragedy, a dramatic comedy, and a farce from among my theatrical works. I readily subscribe to Professor Kilker's logic in making his American selection.

Case for a Rebel was inspired by an actual occurrence. Near Algiers, in 1957, a French worker making common cause with the Algerian insurrection was arrested after he placed a bomb in an electric power plant where he worked. It was conceded at the inquiry that he had regulated the device so that the explosion would only produce material damage. His act belongs in the realm of revolutionary sabotage, not blind terrorism. He was guillotined, not having been allowed to benefit from the measures of clemency granted certain Algerian terrorists. In this climate—emotional with rage and despair—justice was, for him, expeditious.

So as not to disturb the victim's family and, at the request of his friends, I set the scene in Indonesia where the war against Dutch tutelage resembled in many aspects the Algerian war of liberation. I might add that this work would have first been performed in 1960, that is to say, very close to the event that had inspired it. Indeed, Albert Camus had reserved it for the theatre that André Malraux, at the time Minister of Culture, intended to turn over to him. Moreover, it was to discuss this theatre directorship proposal that Albert Camus left Lourmarin at the beginning of January 1960 and set out on his last journey.

My theme is not that of the "scrupulous murderer" who spares his intended victim rather than kill innocent people along with him. In *Case for a Rebel* there is no intended victim. That particular morning Keller goes to the plant with the purpose of harming no one. He is caught at the very moment he changes the device, so anxious is he to protect two workmen who have lingered in the area, rather than to carry out his mission come what may. This act is his undoing. Everyone turns against him. He has betrayed in everyone's eyes. For some he is a traitor to his cause; for others, to his country.

In my own way I have tried to make palpable the circle of hate that inexorably closes in on Keller and transforms his refusal to kill into destiny. If he had only not come back, if he had only let things take their course. It is impossible to live with impunity, however, on the frontiers of the heart.

I have striven to be impartial with each one of my characters and to have them act and speak in accordance with their truth. My aspiration has been to write a tragedy of our time in which Oedipus' cry still rings out, even though the ancient divinities of vengeance are now silent. In the middle of this closed circle Keller himself is also in effect the blasphemer condemned to unhappiness and death.

Inspiration for *The Clock* came from my stays in Naples in the winter and spring of 1944, during the period of the Cassino front. I was a war correspondent and had rented a room from the resident owner of an old building near the Piazza Dante. Occasionally I would go there to rest up between missions. I had then the chance to mix with the people of Naples, to know them, to admire them, and love them for their dignity and courage in adversity. Vanina was born in my imagination as a result of this experience.

Above all we are dealing here with an individual who strongly believes in the value of the human soul and, to better put this attitude to the test, I placed her in the setting of one of those large Mediterranean cities in which the too beautiful sunlight belies genuine poverty and where even the darkest anguish does not necessarily corrupt a noble heart.

To find a model for my Alfieri caused me no more difficulty than finding one for Vanina, so true it is that around us live men of prey who dominate by exploitation of the weak and through corruption. They do not all attain the glory of an Al Capone, for example. But what of it! Lucre and pleasure-bent

minds seldom need submachine guns and may triumph more
hygienically in the luxurious silence of a business office.

I purposely chose these modest long-suffering Mediterranean
people then. If I have given them a few burlesque affectations
or attitudes, it was merely better to point up their vulnerabil-
ity. To embody the revolt against injustice and evil I also purposely chose a young woman, that is to say, an individual
fragile by nature but made strong here by her profound sense of
morality.

This was not, in fact, the only reason that led to my choice.
In my view the highest morals of the present-day world which
are more and more debased or threatened will only be saved by
youth. Vanina symbolizes this idea by her refusal of all that
degrades man or destroys his hope.

So many stern intentions in *The Clock*? readers will say. It is
true I was perhaps about to forget the essential. As a matter of
fact, my play is first of all a story about a fresh and pretty girl,
rather antisocial of character, who believes in love and refuses
compliments that are too direct. Her passion for real feelings
leads her to extremes. That is why, dear Vanina, at the end you
fire the revolver, an action without which tragedies of the heart
would remain just that.

As for *Porfirio*, for me it was a question of writing a farce,
based on my recollections from a stay in South America, for a
young company that I directed in Algeria from 1948 to 1954, Le
Théâtre de la Rue. I adopted this genre for two reasons: first of
all because I very much admired the Arab Theatre of Algiers
founded by Ksentini, Mahieddine, and Djelloul which com-
prised a repertory of satirical farces delightfully paced and col-
orful. Moreover, our troupe included Algerians, Italians,
Spaniards, and Frenchmen, and almost all of them possessed
the qualities of the Commedia dell'arte.

Porfirio takes place then in a small Latin American capital
and was inspired by one of those pronunciamentos fomented
by powerful banana trusts that so often cause so-called military
uprisings of liberation that coincide with their own interests.
But if my General Porfirio is laugh-provoking—I hope he is, of

course—he should not cause certain very real colleagues of his and their bloody deeds to be forgotten, be they in the New World, Europe, Asia, or even the esteemed Idi Amin in Africa.

Indeed, let no one accuse me of having let my imagination run wild. Porfirio orders a parrot shot, but did not Don Tacho Somoza, the president of Nicaragua, have shot a Renault truck, guilty in his mind of high treason for having been built in a Communist factory? And is it necessary to recall to mind the general-president of El Salvador, Hernandes-Martinez, nicknamed the "theosophic butcher," for whom killing an ant was a greater crime than killing a man because "man is reincarnated after his death, whereas the ant disappears forever." By virtue of which concept this lunatic had twenty thousand Indian peasants who were a little too demanding executed. And is it necessary to cite President Gomez of Venezuela who made his decisions according to the movements of a rhinoceros observed over a period of time in his zoological garden? And should Tiburcio Carias of Honduras be mentioned who had his prisoners shot to make it rain? And Leonidas Trujillo of the Dominican Republic? And Haiti's Papa Doc? There are so many more.

All this is to affirm that the whims of my hero never exceed historic reality and that I have even kept for Porfirio his "nice guy" personality which is a trait common to all tyrants, big or little. I might add that the moment he falls in love, he "falls" in the exact sense of the term, that is to say, he is taken out of the action. "Love, the enemy of action," could be, everything considered, another conclusion drawn from this crazy story.

In this concept it seems to me that James A. Kilker justifies the position of this little work after the two more serious plays, since he is convinced, just as I am, that the theatre, beyond the question of genres, is not an imitation of life but life itself.

Introduction

BY JAMES A. KILKER

Outside the community of scholars of French studies, Emmanuel Roblès, an author whose works have not only won a number of literary prizes but have also placed him into the select membership of the Goncourt Academy, is relatively unrecognized in the English-speaking world. Yet this Hispanic Frenchman is quite well known—even popular—in Europe, North Africa, and Latin America. His novels, short stories, and plays, either in the original or in translation, have appeared regularly in the bookstores of these areas for well over twenty-five years. Often, in the case of the theatrical works, publication has followed close on the heels of production. It is safe to say that Roblès's work in general, and his theatre in particular, is better known in Iron Curtain countries than in the United States.

Some of Roblès's novels, when published in English as *The Angry Mountain, Dawn on Our Darkness, Knives, Vesuvius* (to which Henri Peyre wrote an excellent afterword), have met with varying degrees of success. His theatre, however, to this day remains inadequately evaluated on its own merits in English-speaking countries. Although in 1949 it appeared that Roblès's *Montserrat* was about to benefit in New York from circumstances so favorable that they might assure his future dramatic works a forum in the United States, such was not to be the case.

While in Europe in 1948, Lillian Hellman, hearing of the formidable success of *Montserrat*'s double premiere in Paris and Algiers, hastened to the former city to see the play. Pleased with what she saw, she contacted Roblès and signed an agreement with him giving her the rights to do an adaptation of the work. As it turned out, Miss Hellman's version of *Montserrat* proved unfaithful to the spirit of the play, for both form and dialogue were considerably modified. This adaptation of the play failed to score a success on Broadway in 1949 and in England in 1952 when it opened there. Thus *Montserrat*, a play that has continued to meet with universal critical and popular acclaim, has only failed in the English-language rendition which American critics have assumed to be the real Roblès play.

The fortune this play faithfully translated or adapted might have known in English-speaking countries is, of course, a matter of conjecture. Nonetheless, one cannot help but ask the obvious question: What are the ethical limits in adapting a play? And to what extent may an author's reputation and career suffer from a distorted adaptation or an inadequate translation?

Interesting anecdotes could be related about the premiere productions of a number of plays included in Roblès's total theatrical output, without excepting those selected for the present volume. The choice of *Case for a Rebel, The Clock,* and *Porfirio* for inclusion here, however, owes nothing to unusual events attending their premieres, but rather to a desire to present plays of merit reflecting the scope and versatility of Roblès's talent as a playwright. The tragedy, dramatic comedy, and farce offered, first of all, represent diversity of genre. Whereas all three may be performed by most dramatic groups, *Case for a Rebel* was specifically written for the professional stage; *The Clock* and *Porfirio,* for the amateur theater.

A further important factor in the selection of these plays was that they faithfully mirror the author's philosphical stance toward man and society. An internationalist, Roblès has a fraternal commitment to his fellowman that transcends such traditional divisive compartimentalizations as race, nationality, language, religion, and economic or social status. His belief and his faith are in mankind, and any political, societal, or economic force that deprives man of his dignity he finds reprehensible. Throughout his work, Roblès's heroes seek consciously and, at times, unconsciously the inseparable concomitant of human dignity—freedom.

Oppression, the enemy of human freedom and dignity, presents itself in the accompanying plays in several forms. *Case for a Rebel* portrays the oppressiveness of colonialism. In *The*

Clock, oppression is personified by a mafialike, all-powerful landlord in a Mediterranean town who exploits the ordinary and usually supine citizens who happen to be his tenants. Finally, in *Porfirio*, the oppressor is a multinational fruit-producers' trust. Roblès deals with this kind of tyranny in ways which befit the genre of each play; sustained seriousness in his classic-structured *Case for a Rebel*, a mixture of gravity and banter in *The Clock*, and unbridled broad humor in *Porfirio*. But the consciousness of the value of the individual in the mind of the Roblèsian hero is often weighed against the importance of an act of possible benefit to a greater number of human beings. This causes the character considerable anguish, regardless of his or her ultimate decision. Although not thematic, this attitude on the part of Keller in *Case for a Rebel*, when he is afraid of killing two innocent workmen, leads to his capture and sets the stage for the dramatic situation of the play. Similarly Vanina, the female protagonist of *The Clock*, must assure herself that an apartment complex is clear of possible innocent victims before she will consider using an explosive device.

Circumstances surrounding the genesis and productions of the plays included in this volume, while lacking the controversial element earlier ascribed to the Hellman version of the internationally known *Montserrat*, are nonetheless arresting for the insights and the frames of reference they provide for a fuller comprehension of the accompanying texts.

Upon his return from a trip to Japan in the autumn of 1957, Roblès, as he relates in his Foreword, learned of the Algerian terrorist incident that was to play such an important role in prompting the writing of *Case for a Rebel*. Although the occurrence formed the nucleus of the dramatic plot, it did not suffice in itself to encourage him to treat the subject. Living in Algiers, Roblès had personally witnessed the grim aftermath of terrorist activity and it disturbed him deeply. He expressed his feelings on terrorism and terrorists early in 1959 in the following words:

> I have seen a bomb burst near a streetcar stop at rush hour . . . I saw a man enter a Milk-Bar holding by the hand a little five-year-old girl, and return after the assault with a legless child in his arms. I am

haunted by the subject of terrorism. I would like to recover the mentality of the man who throws a bomb, to know what prompts him to
act . . . to cast forth death without knowing whom it will reach.
Camus is urging me to write a play on terrorists, even though he has
already produced *Les Justes*. Because everything is changed . . . [*]

The convergence of these influences resulted, before the year
was out, in a draft that Roblès called "La Vie des autres" [The
lives of others]. But when Camus called his attention to
Simone de Beauvoir's similarly named *Le Sang des autres* [The
blood of others], Roblès revised his title and edited his text as
well to emphasize the important character of his protagonist.
Thus, *Plaidoyer pour un rebelle* (*Case for a Rebel*) denotes
both author and hero's point of view.

When Roblès completed his first version late in 1959, it
looked as if it might be staged almost at once. Camus had requested the script for staging at the Recamier Theatre in Paris,
which André Malraux, as cultural minister of the Fifth Republic, was about to assign him. On December 28, 1959, Camus
again wrote Roblès, stating that he was about to submit the
play to the opinions of some theatre people. A week later, instead of going to discuss plans with Camus concerning the
staging of his new play, Roblès was summoned to a little
schoolhouse in Villeblevin to identify his friend's body. Camus
died January 4, 1960, in an automobile crash.

Ironically, following Camus's death further problems de-
layed the first production of *Case for a Rebel* in French, and it
was the play's successful debut in Germany—first at the Stad-
tebund Theater in Hof, then as a major production of National
German Television, both in 1965—that spurred new production offers for the original French-language version. Brussels,
not Paris, saw the play open on April 13, 1966, at the Théâtre
Royal du Parc to enthusiastic audiences and critics. The Paul
Hervieu Foundation of the Académie Française awarded *Case
for a Rebel* its prize in June of 1966. It was performed in English

---

[*] Denise Bourdet, "Images de Paris," *La Revue de Paris* 66, no. 5 (May 1959):
142.

in the translation presented here at the Unity Theatre, London, in 1974.

After the idea for *The Clock*, first titled "L'Etrange immeuble de la rue Marconi" [The strange building on Marconi street], came to Roblès during his summer stay in France in 1952, he made a draft of the play on the ship taking him back to Algiers. By November he had a completed script, which was scheduled to be performed the next year in Algiers by the Théâtre de la Rue. Shortly before the play went into rehearsal, Colette Chollet, the actress assigned the lead role of Vanina, died in an automobile accident. Although this event entailed cancellation of the stage production, the play was broadcast by Radio-Alger, under the direction of Louis Foucher, in January 1954. Like *Case for a Rebel*, "The Strange Building on Marconi Street" became a hit in a non–French-speaking area before it was staged in France, its area of greatest popularity being Latin America. Indeed, in Buenos Aires the work was even transposed into comic-strip form. Later Roblès gave the present title, *L'Horloge* (*The Clock*), to the work. The first English-language performance of *The Clock*, done from the present translation, was directed as a black theatre production by H. D. Flowers in 1972, at the South Carolina State College, Orangeburg.

Porfirio has enjoyed greater popularity than all other plays by Roblès with the exception of *Montserrat*. A background of political unrest and pronunciamentos that occurred during his first visit to South America in 1945–46 provided his inspiration. Roblès completed *Porfirio* in February 1952, having written it with the Théâtre de la Rue and specific actors in mind. Plans to premiere the play the following month at Menerville, a small city in eastern Algeria, were curtailed when one of the actors was called to military service. *Porfirio* finally opened at the salle Valentin in Algiers in March, 1953. The man to whom Roblès dedicated the play, Paul Grandjean (alias Paul Génès), assumed both the direction and the title role.

Of predominantly Spanish and partly French parentage, Emmanuel Roblès was born in one of the poorer districts of

Oran, Algeria, in 1914. The death of his father, a mason, before Roblès's birth left his mother to be his sole support. Her occupation as a laundress allowed her neither enough time nor money to raise her son as she would have liked. Consequently Roblès became a boy of the streets associating with other "dead-end kids" like himself. But the street did not provide his only education. The young Roblès was an avid reader and an excellent student whose academic achievements gained him scholarships, first at a *collège*, and then at the Écoles Normales of Algiers and Oran. Upon completing his studies at the École Normale in Oran in 1934, Roblès evolved a three-dimensional motif of living consisting of writing, travel, and teaching, a pattern to which he has remained remarkably faithful from that day to this. As he became successful as an author, however, his teaching experiences have taken the form of lectures on an international scale.

Even before leaving the École Normale, Roblès had, during vacations, begun traveling along the coast of North Africa or to Spain by the least expensive means, generally aboard ship in steerage. During this same period he was already contributing to such newspapers as *Oran-Spectacles* and *Oran-Républicain* and, with his savings from this employment, managed to finance partially his first long tour abroad to Communist Russia and Nazi Germany in the summer of 1934. The balance of his expenses was met by the organizer of the tour. Teaching in the Oran–Mers el-Kébir area, beginning in the autumn of 1934, furnished Roblès with his principal livelihood for the next three years. In the summer of 1935, inspired by the example of André Malraux, he visited India, Indochina, and was just beginning a visit of China when he very nearly succumbed as the result of food poisoning.

The year 1937 brought a sudden change of occupation to Roblès when, in September, he was drafted into the French Air Force at Blida, a few miles south of Algiers. Having become fond of the latter city during his first two years of normal school, he commuted there as often as his activities in basic training permitted. Desiring to be in or near Algiers, and knowing that at the end of a month's basic training he might be sent anywhere, Roblès applied—and was accepted—for training as a meteorologist at Agha, a military seaplane base on the waterfront in mid-city, a stone's throw from the University. One afternoon in September, at the Maison de la Culture in Algiers, before being assigned to Agha, Roblès met a young man directing his own theatrical troupe in Fernando Roja's *La Celestina*. This was Roblès's first meeting with Albert Camus.

It was during this period, January 1938, that Roblès published his first novel, *L'Action* [Action], the manuscript of which was finished before he entered military service. As a soldier, however, he continued to write, contributing to *Alger-Républicain*, the crusading newspaper founded by Albert Camus and Pascal Pia. In Algiers too, Roblès's second novel, *La Vallée du paradis* [Valley of paradise], a work Camus had urged him to write, first appeared, in serial form.

In the autumn of 1938 Roblès, although still a soldier, began studying at the University of Algiers, with a specialty in Spanish literature. Immediately after enrolling there, Roblès met a young second-year law student named Paulette Puyade and, the following spring, against a background of international tension and turmoil, the pair married.

Roblès was on premobilization leave in Pau, France, visiting relatives with his wife, in August 1939, when war became imminent. He was immediately ordered back to his unit in Algeria where he was to spend the period of the "phony war," first in staff work as a Spanish-language interpreter, and then again, briefly, in meteorology, having been assured that this change of specialty would result in a more active assignment in Syria. He got no nearer to Syria than the air base at Oued Hamimine, near Constantine, when the armistice between the Pétain government and Germany brought an end to hostilities. Roblès was discharged at Sétif in late July 1940.

After leaving military service, Roblès and his wife were offered positions together at a school in the small town of Turenne (now called Sabra) in the department of Oranie, near Tlemcen and not far from Oran. Here, in relative isolation, Roblès began to write again, notably a one-act play, *Ile déserte* [Desert isle] and a novel, *Travail d'homme* (translated in En-

gland as *The Angry Mountain*), inspired by a dam being con-
structed at nearby Beni-Behdel. Among the few distractions
available to the couple were frequent trips to Oran to visit
Emmanuel's mother, as well as Albert Camus and his wife,
who lived a block away. Camus had returned from France in
December to reside in the home city of his second wife, Fran-
cine. As the true nature of the Vichy government became
apparent, Roblès joined Camus in helping men accused of misdeeds against that regime or the Germans to transit northwest-
ern Algeria to Morocco, en route to Gibraltar. In the spring of
1941, a typhus epidemic broke out in Oranie bringing death to
countless Europeans and Moslems. Among the stricken was
Paulette Roblès. Although she survived (she was sent back to
her mother's home in Algiers to convalesce), Roblès decided,
largely as a result of this experience, to seek a position in a
more healthful environment.

The 1941–42 school year saw Roblès teaching in the Kabyle
mountains of central Algeria, and the following year he succeeded in obtaining a position at the École Normale in Algiers
where he had earlier been a student himself. As soon as he arrived back in the city he participated in a local resistance group
preparing to assist Operation Torch, the allied invasion of
North Africa, although he did not then know the exact date of
the event. It came November 8, when the academic year was
barely underway and shortly after the birth of Roblès's first
child, Paul, who was to be baptized that very day. Only a couple of days after the landing, the Americans, aware of Roblès's
training in meteorology and knowledge of Spanish, offered him
a job with the American Electronic Listening Services which
consisted of monitoring, recording, and translating Spanish
weather broadcasts on a daily basis. Desiring to contribute to
the war effort in some way, Roblès left the École Normale.

Meanwhile the Free French were organizing new armed
forces in North Africa. Roblès was called back into the Air
Force in September 1943. Assigned to intelligence work at first,
he soon learned of a vacancy for a war correspondent with the
French Air Force and applied for it. Although Roblès had no
background or training as a reporter, the commanding general

of the Air Force, General Bouscat, had read *Travail d'homme* which had appeared earlier in the year and won the Grand Prix littéraire de l'Algérie, liked it, and on that basis appointed Roblès war correspondent for the new French Air Force journal, *Ailes de France*.

For the next two years or so Roblès established an enviable record as a reporter in the Mediterranean and European theatres of operation. He witnessed firsthand the invasion of Corsica, participated in the Italian campaign, spent hours in patrol planes and bombers of all sorts. The airfields he haunted were British and American, not just French. And he flew missions with the various commands of the allied air forces. Not surprisingly, Roblès was in several aircraft accidents, but never seriously injured. During this period, too, he first met such literary luminaries as Saint-Exupéry, then serving as a pilot in the French Air Force, André Gide, Philippe Soupault, and others.

The end of the war found Roblès, now a lieutenant, in Germany. Here he continued to write articles and to commute to Paris where *Ailes de France*, now called *Aviation Française*, had been published since shortly after the liberation of that city. With the end of the war Roblès's title changed to press officer.

Before leaving military service Roblès had one last mission to accomplish: accompany as press officer and interpreter the crew of the *Lionel de Marmier*, a giant six-engined flying boat, on a blue-ribbon crossing of the South Atlantic to South America. During the war several of these giant airplanes had been disassembled and the parts hidden from the Germans. Now, near the end of 1945, the *Lionel de Marmier* had been reconstructed. In December, the aircraft flew from Biscarosse to Rio de Janeiro where the crew spent a week. On the next leg of the flight, to Buenos Aires, a propeller blade hurtled into the hull of the plane, killing two passengers, a Brazilian who had boarded at Rio, and a Frenchman. Control cables damaged in the accident and an engine torn from its housing forced the *Lionel de Marmier* to set down on a lagoon near Rocha, Uruguay. After a short stay in Montevideo, and then in Buenos

Aires, Roblès, as the youngest member of the crew, was chosen
to accompany the bodies of the two dead passengers back to
Rio de Janeiro and then to Le Havre aboard the steamship *Dé-
sirade*. The following month, in Paris, Roblès received a military discharge for the second time.

Having made a modest name for himself in the world of letters and acquired experience as a reporter, Roblès was ready to
earn a living by his pen for his family, who had already come to
Paris to join him in 1945. A number of irregularly appearing,
clandestine publications of reduced format had been launched
during the occupation and, with the euphoric enthusiasm born
of liberation, they flourished and blossomed into full-fledged
periodicals. Roblès began to publish regularly in some: *Com-
bat, Gavroche, Les Nouvelles Littéraires, Le Populaire*, in addition to weekly articles in *Aviation Française*, the organ for
which he wrote when in the military. To the earnings he received from these sources he could add the royalties of *Nuits
sur le monde* [The world in darkness], a book of short stories
published by Charlot in Algiers in 1944, and a Paris edition of
Travail d'homme which came off the press in 1945 and was
awarded another prize, the Prix Populiste. Living conditions,
however, were difficult in the Paris of the postliberation period.
Some foodstuffs were in short supply, prices were high, and the
cold, damp Parisian winters exacerbated by a lack of coal, were
reason enough to induce a "man of the sun" with a family to
return to Algeria. Besides, he could continue to contribute to
French journals from abroad. After a month in Pau, en route,
where Roblès completed his new novel *Les Hauteurs de la
ville* [The heights of the city], the family sailed for Algiers in
the late autumn of 1947.

After arrival there Roblès bought a villa in suburban
Bouzaréah on the heights overlooking the city proper. Soon,
the Roblèses' second child, Jacqueline, was born. Roblès accepted a position as literary critic and occasional producer for
Radio-Alger and another as a government functionary in
charge of the book program in *Jeunesse et Sports*. These occu-
pations still left him sufficient time to found a literary journal,

Forge, with the intent of giving an outlet to North African writers for the expression of distinctly *Maghrébin* cultural values or, more accurately, to effect a true French-North African synthesis. With the climate of prejudice and suspicion that prevailed, *Forge* could not, did not, last long. But in its short life-span it published the first texts of such North African writers as Mohammed Dib and Kateb Yacine, to mention but two.

Although Roblès had finished his novel *Les Hauteurs de la ville* in Pau on his way to Algiers, he continued to polish it while completing a play which had been given the provisional title of *Montserrat*. Roblès had already finished the first act of the play early in 1946, shortly after his return from the *Lionel de Marmier* adventure, and had read it to Camus in the course of a social gathering in Paris. Now, in January 1948, Camus, on one of his biannual visits to Algeria to visit his mother, asked Roblès for the manuscript, read it, and took it back to Paris with him. There he presented *Montserrat* to a French government-sponsored agency called Aid to the First Play, established to solicit and judge beginning plays. Of 188 plays submitted, the agency retained two and chose one, *Montserrat* by Roblès, to be staged at the expense of the agency. Camus wired Roblès of the results.

On April 23, 1948, *Montserrat* premiered in Paris and Algiers simultaneously and was a triumph in both versions. Roblès attended the Paris opening at the Théâtre Montparnasse, and his wife the debut in Algiers at the Théâtre du Colisée. Requests for production and translation rights poured in. When he came to Paris for the rehearsals of *Montserrat* and its premiere, Roblès brought along his manuscript of *Les Hauteurs de la ville* which he gave to Charlot, now in Paris, to publish. The novel, presaging with amazing accuracy events that were to occur in Algeria six years later, offers on a more restricted level a parallel to the theme of revolt, liberation, and honor treated with more universality in *Montserrat*. Roblès was honored for both works. For *Montserrat* he received the Prix du Portique as the outstanding dramatist of the year from a jury comprising such distinguished members as André Maurois, Wladimir Porché,

Roger-Ferdinand, Francis Ambrière, Robert Kemp, Gérard Bauër, and Jean Anouilh. *Les Hauteurs de la ville* gained the Prix Fémina for its author.

In 1950, Roblès formed a liaison with the Paris publishing house Editions du Seuil, since Edmond Charlot, his previous publisher, declared himself bankrupt. Seuil acquired the rights to publish several of Roblès's books previously bearing Charlot's imprint and became his publisher. By 1952, Editions du Seuil had appointed Roblès one of its editors and, shortly thereafter, acting on a suggestion of his, the firm created a series of Mediterranean writers, placing it under his direction. The series has been a signal success since its inception, and Roblès himself has been one of the principal contributors.

Although active with Seuil, Roblès preferred to reside in the Algiers area and to work there, commuting to Paris when necessary for business. The violence and disorder he had feared and foreseen in *Les Hauteurs de la ville* for Algeria became a reality. Nonetheless he was at first determined to remain in his homeland. But the sense of physical danger to his family and the realization that it was already too late for meaningful cultural synthesis between Algerians of European ancestry and Algerians of North African origin argued he should leave. The tragic absurd event that forced him to act was the death of his son Paul, in 1958, who accidentally shot himself while playing with a gun procured for protection because of the times.

In 1958, then, Roblès, his wife, and daughter moved back to suburban Paris, to Boulogne. There he has continued to adhere to the same basic pattern of living established earlier in his adult life: writing, extensive traveling, and lecturing. Besides numerous articles, Roblès has published to this date twelve novels, four books of short stories, eight plays, and a book of poetry. Several of his works have been brought to the screen, such as *Cela s'appelle l'aurore* [Dawn on our darkness], made into a film by Luis Buñuel, in 1954. Roblès has become more and more active in television, radio, and films in recent years and, in addition to serving as a consultant, he has adapted some of his own works as well as those of others to these media.

This brief overview attests that Roblès's literary efforts, as well as his greatest overall recognition, have taken place in the areas of the novel and the short story. Still, his theatre must be considered a continuing and vital part of Roblès's creation—important in itself, as well as for the perspective it offers for an assessment of his work as a whole.

It is hoped that the plays selected here, representing variety of genre, subject, and setting, will prompt the reader's further interest in the author together with his literature and theatre.

Plaidoyer pour un rebelle

(CASE FOR A REBEL)

A Play in Four Acts by

Emmanuel Roblès

Translated by James A. Kilker

Cast of Characters

JUDGE HAZELHOFF   *50 to 60 years old*
SCHULTZ   *his assistant, 35 years old*
KELLER   *30 years old*
KAJIN   *Indonesian, 30 years old*
VAN OOSTER   *50 years old*
DR. VAN ROOK   *60 years old*
GUARD   *45 to 50 years old*
KITTY   *Keller's wife, 30 years old*
SÉDARIA   *Indonesian girl, 20 years old*
POLICEMEN, RECORDER   *silent characters*

Copyright ©1973 by James A. Kilker and M. J. Kilker, copyright © 1977 by Southern Illinois University Press.

Caution. Professionals and amateurs are hereby warned that *Plaidoyer pour un rebelle* (*Case for a Rebel*), being fully protected under the copyright law of the United States of America, the British Empire, including the Dominion of Canada, and other countries of the copyright union, is subject to a royalty; and anyone presenting this play without the consent of Southern Illinois University Press will be liable to the penalties by law provided. All applications for the right of amateur or professional production must be made to the Director, Southern Illinois University Press, Post Office Box 3697, Carbondale, Illinois 62901.

This play had its premiere April 13, 1966, at the Théâtre Royal du Parc (Administrator: Roger Reding) in a production directed by Jean-Louis Colmant, and with Roger Dutoit (Keller), Vanderic (Hazelhoff), Michèle Didier (Kitty), M. Mandayi (Kajin), E. Samson (Schultz), L. Charbonnier (Van Rook), and B. Suong (Sédaria). Among the principal televised adaptations are those of J. L. Colmant (Belgian Television, with Roger Dutoit and Vanderic), of Willy van Hemert (Dutch Television, with Jules Hamel and Hetty Verhoogt), and of E. W. Sautter (German Television, with Leonard Steckel and H. Messemer).

*In an Indonesian city during the years 1948–49 at the time of the war
of independence against the Dutch. Single set: Judge Hazelhoff's
office. White walls. To the right of the audience, a door leading to the
interior of the building. At the rear, a double door leading to a corridor going to the outside. To the left, a wide French door facing a
garden of which the tropical foliage can be seen. Near this French
door, Hazelhoff's desk, with a lamp. Near the door on the right,
Schultz's desk, with telephone. At the rear, on each side of the wide
door, two identical pieces of furniture. Through their glass panes
show files and lawbooks. Two rattan armchairs. A large fan on a long
stand. A map of Indonesia on the wall to the right. The set is bright,
sober, neat, without real austerity.*

ACT ONE

SCENE 1

*Schultz, then the Guard and a policeman. Schultz is alone as the
curtain rises. He tries in vain to start the fan, gives up, and wipes his
forehead. At this moment the telephone rings and he returns to his
desk.*

SCHULTZ (*On the phone.*): Yes, speaking. Mr. Hazelhoff hasn't come
    back from the Governor's yet. No, I don't think he will be long.
    Certainly. I won't forget. You can count on me, Your Honor. (*He
    hangs up, nervously mops his brow and picks up the telephone
    again.*) Have the Guard come in.

*A policeman in plain clothes enters through the door on the right,
then the Guard. Someone closes the door after them.*

SCHULTZ (*To the Guard.*): Step forward, now. Come on!

*The Guard complies after a brief glance at the policeman, who re-
mains on duty near the door.*

SCHULTZ (*While consulting a document and in a tone that proves he
    is resuming a previous interrogation.*): So you've admitted you
    never searched the European workers.

GUARD: Never, sir. No, never.

SCHULTZ: Yet your instructions are precise and absolute. You are supposed to search, without distinction, all workers when they come to the plant. Isn't that right?

GUARD: Yes, sir.

SCHULTZ: Why didn't you carry out those orders strictly?

GUARD: That operation always took a lot of time. A large part of the personnel enters the plant through that door.

SCHULTZ: Are you now suggesting limits to your responsibilities?

GUARD: There's another reason, sir.

SCHULTZ: I'm listening.

GUARD: All the Europeans refuse.

SCHULTZ: To be searched?

GUARD: They say it's humiliating for them.

SCHULTZ: Perhaps. But to relieve the Europeans of the search amounts to making the operation still more of a humiliation for the native workers. Isn't that your opinion?

GUARD (*Piteously.*): Yes, sir.

SCHULTZ: And in the present circumstances I don't see what's so humiliating about conforming to a security measure which is in the interest of all personnel. I really don't see it!

GUARD: But sir, who could imagine a European turning against his own and going so far as to place a bomb in the power plant!

SCHULTZ: Precisely that lack of imagination almost cost a great deal.

GUARD: I admit it, sir. I admit I was wrong.

SCHULTZ (*After a reproachful look at the useless fan, quickly wipes his forehead with his handkerchief.*): In any event, if it was so distasteful for you to force the Europeans to comply with being searched, you could at least have kept an eye on them, observed their behavior, their attitudes.

GUARD: But I did! I swear I did!

SCHULTZ: "I did! I did!"—Come on now. You were, like a horse, asleep on your feet.

GUARD: Now, sir!

SCHULTZ: What do you mean "Now sir!" Horses do sleep standing up. Keller was carrying his bomb with a shopping bag in a small box wrapped in newspaper. And that unusual looking package didn't arouse your curiosity, your suspicion!

GUARD: I must have been careless a moment, sir.

SCHULTZ: Careless! That's what they have against you. Call it what you want. All the more since this Keller had a questionable reputation.

GUARD: I didn't know of it, sir, I swear! Why didn't they tell me anything? I'd have particularly . . .

SCHULTZ: (*Consulting some papers.*) Yes, yes. I read here: "Spoke at sympathy rallies in favor of Indochinese militants interned at Poulo Condor . . . Collected funds to aid strikers in Batavia . . ." What do you say to these?

GUARD: Oh, if I had known!

SCHULTZ (*After a silence and in a low, threatening tone.*): But . . . perhaps you were aware?

GUARD: I swear . . .

SCHULTZ: Perhaps you even knew Keller was carrying that bomb . . . yes, yes. You can carry on like a clown. Nothing proves to me you weren't an accomplice. Nothing.

GUARD (*Choking.*): Suspect me? Why sir, I served fifteen years in the Navy!

SCHULTZ: So what! That's no guarantee to me you didn't succumb to the lure of a few beautiful bank notes, for instance.

GUARD: You can ask Admiral Lizer. He was second in command on the destroyer I served on at the time . . .

SCHULTZ: Count on my verifying with Admiral Lizer that you are a monumental idiot. Do you know what your lack of vigilance is going to cost you?

GUARD: I'll lose my job?

SCHULTZ: And serve a sentence of from six months to two years in prison for serious neglect, criminal neglect of your duties.

GUARD: Sir . . .

SCHULTZ: And that only in case it is clearly established that you weren't in collusion with Keller.

GUARD: But . . .

SCHULTZ: That's enough! We're at war. Here, each of us, civilian or military, is a soldier. Our enemies are everywhere. Your job is to stand guard. Who decreed that European workers could be above all suspicion?

GUARD: I explained to you they refused to let themselves be searched . . .

SCHULTZ: And you accepted. You capitulated. It's obvious, you're a stupid jackass. Your responsibility in this affair remains considerable. Whether sooner or later, you'll get your due.

GUARD: But, sir, nothing happened!

SCHULTZ: What do you mean, nothing happened! An individual brings in under your nose, into an establishment you're supposed to protect, a time bomb, a very powerful weapon, and you claim nothing happened?

GUARD: I meant, sir, the bomb didn't explode.

SCHULTZ: Thank God! Or rather, thank the foreman. He had his eyes open—someone you ought to take as an example. If he hadn't had the idea of checking on what Keller was doing in the transformer room, everything would have blown up. And several workers with it.

GUARD: How insane!

Hazelhoff comes in. He appears nervous.

HAZELHOFF: Hello, Schultz. Finished?

SCHULTZ: I will continue in a little while.

He motions to the policeman who pushes the Guard toward the door on the right. Both disappear.

SCENE 2

Schultz, Hazelhoff.

HAZELHOFF (*While leafing through documents on his desk.*): Anything new?

SCHULTZ: No, sir. The Guard is a fool. He doesn't have anything in particular to reveal to us. He seems to be in complete good faith.

HAZELHOFF: I see . . .

He gets up suddenly.

SCHULTZ: Keller refuses to choose a defense attorney.

HAZELHOFF: We'll assign one automatically. Do you know the latest figures? The bomb at the market caused eighteen deaths and injured twenty-seven.

SCHULTZ: A slaughter . . .

HAZELHOFF: I questioned the ordnance people over there. In their opinion this bomb must have resembled fairly closely the one found intact at the factory. Construction the same, same origin.

SCHULTZ: Kajin, right?

HAZELHOFF: Kajin.

SCHULTZ: To think we had him in a camp and let him go.

HAZELHOFF: At the time we had nothing serious against him.

SCHULTZ: He hated us. Wasn't that enough?

HAZELHOFF: Schultz, if we had to intern all Indonesians who hate us

SCHULTZ: It's not a question of that, sir . . .

HAZELHOFF: Just point out to me a people that has shown any love for another dominating them.

SCHULTZ: I'm talking about Kajin. During his internment all reports concerning him show him to be secretive, tough, authoritarian, and with a strange hold over those around him.

HAZELHOFF: There wasn't anything in his file.

SCHULTZ: He belonged to the "Stand Up For Freedom" movement.

HAZELHOFF: Without accepting a responsible position in it. And he left it very quickly.

SCHULTZ: Because he felt the leadership wasn't forceful enough and its positions too moderate.

HAZELHOFF: Moderate? They're demanding total independence!

SCHULTZ: Moderate not so far as the objective is concerned but about the means of attaining it.

HAZELHOFF: Listen, Schultz, I assure you there wasn't much in his file and if they let him go at the time, it was because his behavior in the camp was satisfactory.

SCHULTZ: Who'll believe those few months of confinement were enough to calm down that guy! It's clear now they freed a cruel, ruthless wild animal, all the more dangerous because he lacks neither intelligence nor courage.

HAZELHOFF: And to have him show up in this city where the whole population has learned to keep their mouths shut—even the children!

SCHULTZ: Without counting the fact that most of our informers have been murdered.

HAZELHOFF: Inspector Rijn told me about a lead. It's true that fellow is always off on a lead that almost invariably takes him to the Coral Club bar in front of a whiskey on ice. Let's get to Keller.

SCHULTZ: He's still up in the infirmary. It doesn't seem possible to take him on right away for a real interrogation. His fellow workers in the plant gave him a very thorough going over.

HAZELHOFF: It doesn't matter. We'll hear him anyway. Please bring him down.

SCHULTZ: Very well, sir. I would like to point out that, in accordance with your orders, I had Keller's wife summoned.

HAZELHOFF: Is that the young woman I saw in the waiting room?

SCHULTZ: Yes, sir.

HAZELHOFF: All right. Let's begin with her.

Suddenly Hazelhoff stops walking up and down and brings his hand to his right side grimacing with pain.

SCHULTZ (*Ready to phone to have Mrs. Keller come in.*): Are you in pain, sir?

HAZELHOFF: A small discrete reminder . . .

SCHULTZ: You are not taking care of yourself very thoroughly.

HAZELHOFF: In my case, Schultz, "thoroughly" would mean taking the next plane for Europe and leaving this country for good. At least that's Dr. Rook's opinion. And my wife's . . . (*He sits down.*) By the way, Schultz, is it true you promised to be her chess partner?

SCHULTZ: That's correct, sir.

HAZELHOFF: Are you a good player?

SCHULTZ: Passable, I think.

HAZELHOFF: The game must really captivate you to consent to waste an evening in the company of a doddering old lady.

SCHULTZ: Pardon me, sir, but Mrs. Hazelhoff is very witty and plays chess admirably.

HAZELHOFF: That's what I mean: in spite of appearances, this city is dreadfully lacking in entertainment. Come on, have the young woman come in.

SCHULTZ (*Picking up the phone again.*): Hello? Sergeant? Mrs. Keller.

SCENE 3

Hazelhoff, Schultz, Kitty. Kitty enters timidly. She watches the door close again behind her.

HAZELHOFF (*A curt gesture of greeting.*): Madam . . . Would you please be seated . . .

KITTY: Thank you.

She sits down.

HAZELHOFF: I summoned you here to ask certain questions about Johann Keller, your husband . . .

KITTY (*In a spurt.*): How is he? Will I be able to see him soon?

HAZELHOFF: You will see him.

KITTY: This morning's papers say he was lynched by the workers in the courtyard of the plant.

HAZELHOFF: "Lynched" is a very strong word. Let us say he was somewhat roughed up . . .

KITTY: The police who came to search my place during the night claimed he hadn't regained consciousness . . .

HAZELHOFF: Just as exaggerated . . . I can reassure you on his condition.

KITTY: Why don't you authorize me to see him right away?

HAZELHOFF: Be patient.

KITTY: Perhaps because he's been tortured!

HAZELHOFF: No, Mrs. Keller, he wasn't tortured.

KITTY: Is he here? In this building?

HAZELHOFF: On the second floor, in the infirmary. May I in my turn ask you some questions?

KITTY: Excuse my emotions, sir . . .

HAZELHOFF: You have been married to Keller for four years, isn't that right?

KITTY: Yes. I met him after his release from a Japanese camp.

HAZELHOFF: Was he already working at the power station?

KITTY: No. I was a linen maid on a passenger ship liner, the *Breda*. Keller worked on shore here for the same company.

HAZELHOFF: It was after your marriage then that he began at the plant?

KITTY: Yes, because of the higher salary. And because he refused to let me continue in a job that kept us apart several days a month. The *Breda* was on the Singapore run.

HAZELHOFF: His fellow workers say he is rather uncommunicative by nature.

KITTY: He's not very outgoing, if that's what they mean. But he is good-hearted. I don't know where he could have gotten the idea for that bombing attempt.

SCHULTZ (*Suddenly.*): You knew he was closely interested in politics?

KITTY: Yes. But with me he didn't speak much about those things.

SCHULTZ: He certainly must have gotten around to referring to this war in front of you?

KITTY (*Careful.*): He would say the colonies were condemned to disappear in our time, that it was the evolution of history . . .

SCHULTZ: What people did he see? (*Since she hesitates.*) He had friends!

KITTY (*Still on her guard.*): Yes, of course . . .

SCHULTZ: Natives?

KITTY: Natives, Europeans . . . (*Sharply.*) But I didn't know them.

SCHULTZ: Still, they must have met together at times at your place? Did you receive them?

KITTY: Never . . . Keller never brought them together at home. I didn't like that. I told him so.

HAZELHOFF: Last night they found some rather special books at his place. Political treatises, brochures, reviews . . .

KITTY: He read a lot. He said it's a worker's duty to educate himself.

SCHULTZ: How did he get hold of these works?

KITTY: I don't know.

SCHULTZ: A certain number of them are either forbidden or unavailable.

KITTY: I couldn't tell you.

SCHULTZ (*Ironically.*): Really?

KITTY: These books and publications didn't interest me . If it was up to me, I would have thrown them away.

HAZELHOFF (*Getting up suddenly.*): I concede that. Now, Madam, listen to me carefully. I am going over some facts that are probably already familiar to you. Yesterday afternoon, around four o'clock, the foreman of the workshop where your husband works became intrigued by his attitude and behavior. He spied on him and finally discovered a bomb in the center of the main installation that controls all operations of the power station. Keller was arrested. And he has admitted his crime.

KITTY: His crime! He didn't kill anybody!

HAZELHOFF: Two days earlier, a bomb of the same construction, according to the experts, exploded as you know in the middle of the market. The morgue and the hospital are overflowing with the victims.

KITTY (*Her face in her hands.*): My God . . .

SCHULTZ: We aren't asking you to talk against your husband but to help us, if possible, to find his accomplices. I suppose you don't approve of acts of this kind.

Kitty shakes her head no.

HAZELHOFF: You didn't want to answer a certain question but, everything considered, it's not important. We have a list of the people you actually had at your home. Not one suspect among them. The dangerous people, Keller met away from home.

SCHULTZ: He often came home rather late at night, didn't he?

KITTY (*Observing him to guess whether the question conceals a trap.*): Often, as a matter of fact . . .

SCHULTZ: He'd never tell you where he was coming from? His reasons for coming in so late?

KITTY: He told me whatever he wanted . . .

SCHULTZ: And you didn't try to find out anymore about it?

KITTY: It was difficult with him.

SCHULTZ: Why?

Kitty shrugs her shoulders.

HAZELHOFF: And nothing even in the rare remarks he might have made alerted you concerning this attempted bombing?

KITTY: No.

SCHULTZ: Did he completely approve of the rebellion?

KITTY: I don't know. But at the outset he felt there was injustice and exploitation. The poverty around us affected him deeply. He's of very poor origin. Poverty for him is the greatest of evils that destroy the soul.

HAZELHOFF: Did he say it that way?

KITTY: Yes.

HAZELHOFF: Exactly that way?

KITTY: Yes. You know, he received a religious education in his childhood.

SCHULTZ (*Smirking.*): Curious results.

HAZELHOFF: I can conceive that Keller kept you out of his political involvements, that he hid his militant activities from you, but you lived too close to him not to be aware of his behavior, his changes of attitude or mood.

KITTY: He could be very secretive.

HAZELHOFF: Even with you?

KITTY: Especially with me.

HAZELHOFF: Just explain yourself!

KITTY: If I'd suspected a plan like that, do you think I'd have done nothing? Don't you think I'd have tried everything to keep him from it? I'd have done anything. I'd have screamed! Oh, would I have screamed!

SCHULTZ (*After a silence.*): Did he sometimes say the name Kajin in your presence?

KITTY: No, never . . .

HAZELHOFF: Kajin is a terrorist leader. It is certain your husband saw him often.

KITTY: My husband is not a blood-thirsty man. How can you contend . . .

SCHULTZ: All the same, he did place a bomb in the power plant. For a man with so little taste for blood, you'll have to agree, he was preparing quite a massacre!

KITTY: They threatened him. I'm sure they made him do it under threat!

SCHULTZ: We shall see.

KITTY: He could only have acted under pressure. He'd never have freely agreed to such a horrible act!

SCHULTZ: He'll be interrogated on that point.

KITTY: What are his chances?

SCHULTZ: That's the business of the court.

KITTY: But the bomb didn't explode!

SCHULTZ: Not because of him. It was the foreman's vigilance that just barely averted that catastrophe!

KITTY: But there weren't any victims!

SCHULTZ: We are talking about a criminal act carried out in its initial stages. It is punishable under the law just as if it had been completed.

HAZELHOFF: You said awhile ago, Madam, that Keller could be very secretive.

KITTY: Yes.

HAZELHOFF: And you added: "Especially with me." Why?

KITTY (*Very troubled*.): Since the beginning of all these events something was . . . had changed between us.

HAZELHOFF: How do you mean?

KITTY: He had become . . . more distant. That's the exact word. More distant. And the night before last . . .

HAZELHOFF: The night before last? Go on, speak . . .

Here, the lights go out. It is night at Kellers home, the eve of the bombing attempt.

SCENE 4

Kitty, Keller. Kitty has not moved. With the change of lighting she is under a vertical spotlight that sets her apart. Off to the side, the other two personages. Kitty has turned toward the French door. She is watching Keller approach and come into the room, that is to say, into his own home.

KELLER: Hello . . .

KITTY (*Coldly.*): Hello . . .

KELLER: It's really humid!

KITTY: It's the season . . .

KELLER: Coming here I saw soldiers searching houses behind the plant.

KITTY (*Purposefully.*): They're probably hunting down terrorists . . .

KELLER: They put the women against the wall, beat the men . . . Even the old ones. Slapped and hit with rifle butts!

KITTY: Yes . . .

KELLER: As a joke the police were scaring those unfortunate people, assuring them they would be shot on the spot. I was ashamed . . .

KITTY: That's a nice reaction.

KELLER: Why do you talk like that? Am I boring you with this story?

KITTY: Not at all! I understand perfectly that the sight upset you. Do you want to have some dinner?

KELLER: No.

KITTY: At least some fruit?

KELLER: Not hungry. I hope you had dinner without waiting for me.

KITTY: I snacked.

KELLER: You look strange.

KITTY: I'm glad you noticed. Am I allowed to tell you you look strange too?

KELLER: Don't bother about me.

KITTY: You can be satisfied. I've made up my mind to do as you say.

KELLER: Which means?

KITTY: The *Breda* came into port this morning.

KELLER: And you couldn't resist going to see it.

KITTY: That's right, I didn't resist. And I wonder, really, what could have strengthened my resistance.

KELLER: You met Walling?

KITTY: Yes.

KELLER: Ah . . . How did the interview go?

KITTY: What a lot of questions, Johann. Generally what I do in your absence doesn't seem to worry you.

KELLER: All right! So? Good old chief steward Walling? . . .

KITTY: He's putting me back on the roster as a linen maid.

KELLER: Is that what he offered you?

KITTY: No. I asked for it.

KELLER: Oh . . . You want to leave?

KITTY: The *Breda* is sailing for Amsterdam in three days. It's supposed to be converted into a hospital ship.

KELLER: You've already signed up?

KITTY: Not yet. But I am going to. I have an appointment at the Company office.

KELLER: It's serious then?

KITTY: Completely.

KELLER: I admit I wasn't expecting that bit of news.

KITTY: It's not a bit of blackmail on the part of an abandoned wife. You can believe that.

KELLER: I do believe you. But I don't understand the decision.

KITTY: Does it really surprise you?

KELLER: Everything wasn't going for the best between us, I admit . . . But as a reason for separating!

KITTY: It's just that I've had enough! I've repeated it to you often. I've had enough of this life you make me lead. Enough of waiting for you to come home, of being attendant on your whims; enough of this stinking city! too much of being alone; of being useless. I feel like I'm rotting away in some kind of slime.

KELLER: You did, however, agree to live here with me.

KITTY: Yes, with you. Not alongside. When I met you, you inspired my trust. You seemed solid. And then, linen maid on an ocean liner . . . I was beginning to tire of that life. I wanted to stop. I mean, no longer be alone. To belong . . .

KELLER: And you want to take to the sea again?

KITTY: Why do you pretend not to understand?

KELLER: Are you that unhappy?

KITTY: I'm not happy.

KELLER: It seems to me you have everything. This house . . .

KITTY: Listen, Johann . . . I refuse to live like these native concubines who are refused nothing in the way of adornment and whose only duties are to prepare meals and spread their thighs.

KELLER: I have never treated you as a kept woman, Kitty. I have treated you as a companion. But understand that a momentous tragedy is taking place in this country and we are in the midst of extraordinary events that may transform the world!

KITTY: Shooting every day, bodies on sidewalks, bombs that explode under foot! I don't find anything exalting in all that!

KELLER: In spite of everything, I thought you were closer to me. I didn't know things had gone so far.

KITTY: I've been waiting patiently.

KELLER: And today the *Breda*'s arrival made you make up your mind?

KITTY: The arrival of the *Breda* made me admit to myself that the time spent in your house was just another stopover at a port that lasted a little longer than a lot of others. It's a revelation painful to a person who had illusions when getting off the boat. I was an exhausted swimmer reaching dry land. I am returning to the water without even having regained my strength.

KELLER: You're being hard on me, Kitty. But I didn't understand, I admit it.

KITTY: Too late, Johann. The *Breda* is waiting for me. It's a prison too, but without shooting or puddles of blood.

KELLER: I'm truly sorry you made that decision, Kitty. We could go on, try again another way.

KITTY: Think a moment. Why would you give up your ideas and a way of life you like? The police will become interested in your activities one of these days and this momentous tragedy, as you put it, for you, will only have a jail cell as a setting.

KELLER: Kitty, don't destroy anything yet.

KITTY: Everything is already destroyed. I don't very well see what could be saved.

KELLER: You don't want to understand.

KITTY: Of course I do. You want to transform the world!

KELLER: Why the irony? It really can be transformed! Be made less cruel, less unjust! It's not the dream of a lunatic or even an enlightened fool!

KITTY: One of my uncles was a pastor. He made me wary of those who only think of bringing about happiness for all of humanity while neglecting those living very close to them.

KELLER: When I was eighteen, I worked in the electric shop of a firm belonging to a rich shipowner in Amsterdam. A valuable piece of jewelry disappeared and I was accused. The police beat me to make me confess. Afterwards the jewel was found.

KITTY: So?

KELLER: My explanations were vain. Words—mine—didn't have any meaning, I guessed that. I was an ordinary worker accused by a powerful man. I was like a Jew before the SS, like a colonial before his masters. No communication, no language possible. In advance, guilty!

KITTY: Because the police acted improperly and didn't do their duty!

KELLER: On the contrary. The police are always on the side of the rich. And the police who questioned me were completely convinced, sincerely convinced, thàt I was a thief. "Come on, confess and we won't do anything to you. Confess and we'll leave you alone. Don't be stubborn. Where'll it get you, boy? Besides, you're the only one who could have done it. Come on, own up: you let yourself be tempted; you needed money! We know you don't make a good living. Admit you couldn't take your eyes off that jewel! We'll take it all into consideration as well as your confession!"

KITTY: And did you confess?

KELLER: Of course I confessed, Kitty! What do you think? That I'm a

hero? That I can take it for long tied by my forearms twenty cen-
timeters from the ground? The police were promised a nice reward.
You could be sure of their zeal!

KITTY: That's horrible, Johann!

KELLER: Horrible? Just look around you. All the millions of people who
live on plantations. Born to work hard and be badly paid. Colonial
manpower! It's nothing. It's understood that, if need be, they'll
admit they're despicable, that they're guilty. Of course I confessed.
Everything! I admitted everything. Yes. But that was insufficient
because on one point I couldn't give any details. That's right! I
didn't know where the jewel was. I'd forgotten where I had hidden
it. Or whom I sold it to. So then they twisted my arm; they inflated
my belly with salt water and hung me by my wrists. They promised
me other amusing pastimes!

KITTY: Johann!

KELLER: Mind you, the jewel had been found early the next morning,
but the owner waited until noon to telephone the police. So I paid
extra. Five hours extra. And no one apologized! What a joke! They
told me if I filed charges they'd prosecute me for my false confession, for my contempt of the judicial system! There again I was
guilty, because I should have had the invincible courage of the innocent to resist, without confessing, until death! That's right, until
death!

He starts to leave.

KITTY: Where are you going, Johann?

KELLER: To see some colleagues. I too have had enough of being alone!

KITTY: But the curfew . . .

KELLER: The curfew is for the natives. Not for whites. The patrols do
differentiate. All the same, I do belong to the race of the masters!
And the masters extend their logic to the point of making themselves respected here even in the persons of those whites they despise!

He exits.

SCENE 5

*Kitty, Hazelhoff, Schultz. The light has returned. We are again in
Hazelhoff's office. Kitty's interrogation resumes.*

HAZELHOFF: At what time did he come home?

KITTY: Rather late.

SCHULTZ: Did you hear him?

KITTY: Yes. But he stayed downstairs. He slept downstairs. He didn't join me in our bedroom.

HAZELHOFF: And you didn't think of going downstairs to him, to talk to him again?

KITTY: What good would it have done? We had said everything. My decision was firm. He had moved me with his memories but I resisted all feelings of pity. I really wanted to go away, settle down in my own country, live another life.

SCHULTZ: And the next day?

HAZELHOFF: That is to say: yesterday morning?

KITTY: He left for the plant at the usual time.

SCHULTZ: How did he act?

KITTY: He seemed preoccupied. I attributed that to our scene of the night before.

HAZELHOFF: He talked to you?

KITTY: No.

SCHULTZ: Yet you saw him?

KITTY: I watched him from my window but I didn't let myself go downstairs.

SCHULTZ: You intended to go to the *Breda* without saying anything to him?

KITTY: Not at all. I had made up my mind to say good-bye properly. However, it seemed to me useless for us to begin hurting each other again before departure time.

HAZELHOFF: Here, Madam, is what followed—as far as he is concerned. After leaving the house he went to see the individual who was supposed to give him the weapon: a bomb with a clock-mechanism detonator and of enormous destructive power.

KITTY: I just can't manage to account for his behavior. There wasn't any hatred in him. Not even an enthusiasm strong enough to motivate an act of that kind!

SCHULTZ: Do you think your breaking off that night could have influenced his mind in any way?

KITTY (*With bitterness.*): Oh, no . . . Perhaps, deep inside, he accepted it with relief. In a way, I freed him . . .

HAZELHOFF: Let's be explicit: it is clear to you that your breaking off, in a word, would not have induced him to act.

KITTY (*Flustered.*): What are you trying to make me say?

HAZELHOFF: Nothing more, Madam. You may go.

KITTY: When will they let me see him?

HAZELHOFF: Tomorrow, right here, ten o'clock. I hope it will be possible.

KITTY: It's not certain, then?

HAZELHOFF: Just come back tomorrow. You will know in time.

KITTY (*Hesitating near the door.*): I didn't, at least, say anything that could add to his misfortune?

SCHULTZ: Put your mind at ease, Madam. But nothing you said can help him either.

KITTY (*Staring at him.*): My God, how you hate him!

She exits.

SCENE 6

Hazelhoff, Schultz.

HAZELHOFF: Your impression, Schultz?

SCHULTZ: An actress! She acted bewildered but said only what she wanted to say. She was watching herself.

HAZELHOFF: You don't believe her story?

SCHULTZ: My job and my experience, which is rather short, do not allow me, sir, to believe in the complete sincerity of the individuals who appear before me.

HAZELHOFF (*Smiling.*): All right, all right. And what do you think she is hiding from us?

SCHULTZ: I couldn't say anything for sure.

HAZELHOFF: That Keller really kept her out of his activities has been substantiated. As regards the *Breda*, it's easy to verify.

SCHULTZ: I will do it, sir.

HAZELHOFF: In my opinion, we won't get anything out of Mrs. Keller. She is the kind of woman who, after having been buffeted around by life, wants a husband completely to herself, a spotless house with polished furniture, and, perhaps, a lot of children. A carefree middle-class existence. Just the opposite of what Keller offered her.

SCHULTZ: To neglect such a pretty woman for politics and subversive activities. He was taking some risks.

HAZELHOFF: In a word, he was taking them all.

SCHULTZ: The picture Mrs. Keller gave us seems quite a good likeness. He's the typical militant, narrow in his views and tough, able to carry out the most absurd orders without emotion and without questions.

HAZELHOFF: I am of a different opinion. An elemental, pretentious rebel. An embittered man!

SCHULTZ: We shall see, sir.

HAZELHOFF: That's right. Please have him brought in.

He opens a file.

SCHULTZ (*Telephoning.*): Sergeant Krelt? Hello? Yes. Right away. No, no handcuffs.

He hangs up.

HAZELHOFF: This damnable pain won't go away.

SCHULTZ: What does your doctor say, sir?

HAZELHOFF (*In a good mood.*): Rook? Doctor Rook? That filthy opium addict? Why he doesn't give one damn.

He still has his nose in the file.

SCHULTZ: If you are not satisfied, why not change doctors?

HAZELHOFF: He's an old companion. Then too, he interests me.

SCHULTZ: As an opium smoker?

HAZELHOFF: A physician addicted to opium looks at his patients the way you look at the pictures on a movie screen. At the cinema we are sometimes moved without forgetting that we are only seeing an illusion. That's the way it is with Van Rook. He is following the progression of the illness in me. This progression, however slow it may be, seems to have for him all the charm that the chase in a "Western" has for others.

SCHULTZ: I would say you are caricaturing him.

HAZELHOFF: Barely, Schultz, barely. Rather than judge men, he often advises me, I should go off by myself to the seashore, "empty my mind of all poison," as he says, and "welcome in meditation the immobile and colorless essence of the universe."

SCHULTZ: He preaches abnegation to others yet he goes into the bush to take care of the wounded.

HAZELHOFF (*Smiling and without raising his head.*): The contradiction is only apparent. Van Rook's thought goes forward in swirls rather than in a straight line. (*He sits up straight.*) Anyway, how do you know he is in contact with the guerrillas?

SCHULTZ: It has been rumored . . .

HAZELHOFF: Let it be rumored, Schultz. The police were unable to learn anything about this matter. Little bits of slander. Feelings have been aroused to the point that people are angry with him for continuing to take care of the natives.

SCHULTZ: And when he receives an injured man he neglects to inform us if the visitor and his wound are suspicious to him.

HAZELHOFF (*Smiles.*): You would like to turn Rook into your informer? A funny thought. (*He nervously thumbs through some sheets.*) Ah, here's the report by the ordnance people who defused the bomb. I find a detail . . . an important detail!

SCHULTZ: On what, sir?

HAZELHOFF (*Nervous.*): Please ask them to hurry up a little more with Keller.

SCHULTZ: All right, sir.

HAZELHOFF: That fellow has some surprises in store for us!

Schultz goes out. Hazelhoff continues reading with a keen interest at the

CURTAIN

ACT TWO

SCENE 1

Hazelhoff, Schultz, Keller, policemen. As the curtain goes up, Hazelhoff is seated at his desk and is reading the ordnance report. The door opens. Schultz, a policeman, and then Keller enter, then a second policeman, and the recording clerk, who goes to sit down at Schultz's table.

SCHULTZ: Here is Keller, sir.

Keller comes forward slowly. He is dressed as he was in the first act and drags his leg a little.

HAZELHOFF: Step forward. Step forward, then . . .

Keller obeys. The policemen remain on duty behind the door through which they entered.

HAZELHOFF (*To Keller.*): Are you suffering?

KELLER: It's bearable.

HAZELHOFF: Sit down.

Hazelhoff turns around Keller as if wondering where to begin the interrogation. Finally he returns to his desk, picks up a document.

HAZELHOFF: You are Keller, Johann, born March 27, 1918, in Amsterdam, electrical worker, married, no children.

KELLER: Yes.

HAZELHOFF: And you admit having placed a time bomb yesterday afternoon in the electric plant where you were employed . . .

KELLER: Yes.

HAZELHOFF: You didn't act on your own initiative.

KELLER: No.

HAZELHOFF: Who procured the bomb for you?

KELLER: A comrade.

HAZELHOFF: His name?

KELLER: I don't know.

HAZELHOFF: Come on now! I hope you don't intend to maintain that an unknown person asked you to put an explosive device in the power station and that you agreed off-handedly, the way you might to do a favor for someone, like that.

KELLER: I don't know the name of the man who gave me the bomb.

SCHULTZ: Fine. (*He takes a photograph out of his drawer.*) In this photo you can see several plant workers posing. You are next to this fellow. (*He points out a face on the photo and puts it before his eyes.*) Do you contend you don't know him? He's holding you by the shoulder, nevertheless!

KELLER: Him, I know him.

SCHULTZ: Kajin, correct?

KELLER: Yes, that's his name all right, but he's not at all involved in this affair.

SCHULTZ: Wait. The bomb found intact in the power station—your bomb, if you will—was of the same construction as some others attributed, without a doubt, to Kajin and discovered recently. What do you say to that?

KELLER: I don't know who made the bomb.

SCHULTZ: Wait again! The case containing your bomb bears penciled instructions for setting it off. And these instructions are indisputably in Kajin's handwriting.

HAZELHOFF: Perhaps you don't know the name of the accomplice who gave you the weapon, but you know its source without any possible doubt.

KELLER: No. I agreed to act out of conviction, without asking for details.

HAZELHOFF: What discretion! It does strengthen an attitude in case of interrogation, doesn't it?

SCHULTZ (*Gruffly.*): Let's get it over with, Keller! Time is short. It's useless to continue this game: two of your lookouts fell into our hands. We made them talk! Listen here . . . The meeting with Kajin took place in an abandoned house, a house behind the gasworks, precisely the fourth one going down toward the river. Is that enough detail for you?

KELLER: I don't have anything to say to you.

SCHULTZ: That's just where you're mistaken! And there is this: you arrived ahead of time. Kajin joined you accompanied by a girl. Isn't that exact? But perhaps you don't know her name? Do you know it? Answer!

KELLER (*Overwhelmed but still resisting.*): I don't know what you're talking about!

SCHULTZ: You're lying! You know very well whom I'm referring to. The girl's name is Sédaria. Kajin gave you her name himself. Correct?

KELLER: Since you know so much . . .

SCHULTZ: Stop the playacting, Keller! We know even more. (*He draws near Keller.*) For instance . . . that it was this Sédaria who planted the bomb in the market!

Silence.

HAZELHOFF: Your obstinacy is useless and your reticence, ridiculous. You are going to tell us about that scene immediately. We already know the essentials.

KELLER: In that case, what's the use?

SCHULTZ: Once more, Keller, don't be a fool. It's not a question of denunciation! We've shown you that. We want to know in what light you ought to be considered.

KELLER: I'm against all colonial systems.

HAZELHOFF: And this stand led you to join Kajin's terrorist group?

KELLER: No. I didn't know a thing about that group. Moreover, it's on the fringe of the Insurrectional Organization.

HAZELHOFF: But approved by it!

KELLER: Tolerated . . .

HAZELHOFF: Let's get back to the subject. Kajin, then, called you together. How? We know.

SCHULTZ: He had you informed that it was urgent for him to see you, and you agreed to contact him. But did you suspect the exact purpose of this meeting?

KELLER: I thought it was about an underground printing press. In the days when Kajin worked with me at the power plant, he often spoke to me about it.

8 8 9 8 3

College of St. Francis Library
Joliet, Illinois

HAZELHOFF: So you left your wife that night after a rather bitter dispute.

Silence. Keller is very surprised.

KELLER: So you know that too?

SCHULTZ (*Pitilessly.*): We even know the name of the boat she was getting ready to take to return to Europe: the *Breda*.

HAZELHOFF (*With good-natured irony.*): You see?

KELLER: Just what could she have told you?

SCHULTZ: It's you who are to answer our questions, Keller.

HAZELHOFF: You were the first, then, to enter the house and you waited.

KELLER (*As in a dream.*): Yes, I waited . . .

SCHULTZ: You turned on the lights first!

KELLER (*Glancing at him briefly.*): I turned on the lights first and I waited in front of the door . . .

SCENE 2

Keller, Kajin, Sédaria. As in the first act Hazelhoff and Schultz have sat down somewhat toward the rear. Keller has remained in his place under a lighting that isolates him. Moonlight through the bay window on the left. Kajin appears first, dressed in worker-blue. He is bareheaded. Sédaria follows him and turns around often as if keeping watch on the rear.

KAJIN (*Surprised.*): Already here?

KELLER: Why not?

KAJIN: As a matter of fact, why not? (*He designates his companion.*): Sédaria . . .

KELLER: Hello.

SÉDARIA: Hello.

KAJIN: Been waiting for us long?

KELLER: Half an hour . . .

SÉDARIA: Were you so impatient to see Kajin?

KELLER (*Who has just lit a cigarette.*): Let's say, rather, that I had enough of staying around my place.

SÉDARIA: By your wife?

KELLER: By my wife. Between two evils, right? . . . And now that we're all here, what's it about?

KAJIN: I'll tell you; but I hope you were sufficiently careful coming here?

KELLER: Nothing suspicious anywhere along the way.

KAJIN: Meet any patrol?

KELLER: Only one. Everything went well. So now?

KAJIN: You're going to see.

He takes out a paper.

KELLER: Printing press?

KAJIN: No. It doesn't concern a printing press. (*He has spread his paper on the table.*) Recognize this?

KELLER: The power station.

KAJIN: Right. Here, the transformer room.

KELLER: Exactly.

KAJIN: Tomorrow evening, five o'clock, all that has to blow up.

KELLER: At least you get straight to the point.

KAJIN: Five o'clock sharp.

KELLER: Meaning a complete breakdown for quite a few days?

KAJIN: The number of days doesn't matter much.

KELLER: What's the point in destroying the thing?

SÉDARIA: Do you have any objections?

KAJIN: The machines and the important installations are indicated in red. In blue, the pillars. The courtyard is to the left.

KELLER: Exactly.

KAJIN: Placing the bomb here will bring about maximum damage.

KELLER: And there's this pillar. If it gives way, most of the roof will collapse.

KAJIN: It'll give way. The weapon is very powerful.

KELLER: Is it possible to know why you want to destroy the plant?

KAJIN: Wait. No questions for the moment. Here are the two entrances. The guards search the native workers. Never the Europeans.

KELLER: But they still have sharp eyes.

KAJIN: The guard at this door here is the least strict.

KELLER: Incorruptible, I warn you.

KAJIN: He'll let a European worker carrying a package through, however, without asking to see anything.

KELLER: Probably.

KAJIN: I thought of you for this job.

KELLER: I was beginning to suspect so.

KAJIN: You spoke to me one day about unconditional solidarity.

KELLER: Certainly . . .

SÉDARIA: Words are not just words.

KELLER: Who ever said the contrary, lovely!

SÉDARIA: Will you change your manner?

KAJIN: That's enough!

KELLER (*To Kajin.*): Charming tigress! But couldn't you send her elsewhere to do her nails?

KAJIN: Do you agree?

KELLER: Just a moment. There are questions I wanted to ask you.

KAJIN: Now I can listen.

KELLER: Workers could be in that room at five o'clock.

KAJIN: Take care so that they see nothing.

KELLER: Easy to say. But there's something else.

KAJIN: What?

KELLER: Maybe no one will be there when I plant the bomb, but maybe there will be someone at the time it goes off.

KAJIN: It has to go off at five o'clock on the dot.

KELLER: Why?

KAJIN: At five o'clock four of our people are to be judged by the military tribunal. Good men. We've found no better way of protesting, of making our presence and vigilance felt, and of helping our comrades' morale a bit too.

SÉDARIA (*Vindictively.*): Not counting the refrigerators going off in the beautiful houses of the whites and the electric fans not working!

KELLER (*Ironically.*): That's true. Tepid drinks and perspiration will also make the rich planters do some thinking.

SÉDARIA: Anything that makes them think is good: lack of comfort as well as lack of security.

KELLER (*To Kajin.*): Your plan suits me. But coming back to my remark: there's a risk the explosion will kill some people.

KAJIN: It's only a risk.

SÉDARIA: And since you're risking a lot yourself as well, your conscience should be relieved.

KELLER: Relieved. If some of my friends are turned into mincemeat through my fault, I won't be relieved at all!

SÉDARIA: It's not you, it's not us who would be guilty! It's those who oppress us!

KELLER: That's certainly true.

SÉDARIA: We don't exist! We are only used as beasts of burden. We've got to prove we exist, that we want to exist. We've got to act at all costs! Without weakness. They make us do it. It's the planters and their accomplices who drive us to do it.

KELLER: Have you finished your routine?

KAJIN (*Indulgent.*): She was arrested last week and the soldiers of the Legion used her.

SÉDARIA (*Indignant.*): Why are you telling him that? There was no need! And if he lacks courage, we shall see without him.

KAJIN (*Exasperated.*): Let's finish. (*To Keller, changing his tone.*) If there are any victims it will be a misfortune, a real misfortune. But during the war, the Allies with their air raids over Holland and Belgium also caused victims among their own friends. The Soviets, when they attacked their own occupied cities, were in danger too of striking their fellow countrymen. You have to know what you want.

KELLER: I know, I know—still the story of the omelet! All right. Your fireworks suit me. For the rest, I'll manage. Who are the four comrades?

KAJIN: Two in charge of propaganda, one officer, one supply man.

KELLER: Poor devils. Young?

KAJIN: The oldest is scarcely thirty.

KELLER (*After a silence.*): Another question.

KAJIN: Yes, but hurry up.

KELLER: The bomb in the market . . . was it you?

KAJIN: Don't get involved in that.

KELLER: Because I'm willing to admit political assassination. But that slaughter!

KAJIN: Let's get back to business. It's already late.

KELLER: Lenin condemned terrorism!

SÉDARIA: A noble mind! I admire him.

KELLER: He truly loved the people. These blind acts of violence are barbarian. The people alone suffer the consequences.

KAJIN: The people! We are the people!

SÉDARIA (*With a sudden harshness.*): And we are in slavery! Each of us, at all hours, ought to feel concerned by this war. Involved in this tragedy. No onlookers! That's too simple.

KELLER (*Coolly.*): Tell me, young lady, it wouldn't be because a platoon of legionnaires raped you that the whole earth must pay for this misfortune! Massacres right and left won't give you back your virginity.

SÉDARIA: You, you are for our cause provided everything is accomplished without your losing yours! The virginity of soul of those who don't kill!

KELLER: Little girl, I fought against the Japanese fascists. And not in the supply services! And I swear that had an aspect different from playing at pulling legs off children the way you pull legs off flies.

He moves toward her.

SÉDARIA (*Threatening.*): Don't come near me. Stay where you are!

She has plunged her hand into her pocket.

KELLER (*Disgusted.*): A crazy girl! If she were supposed to kill me, she'd do it.

KAJIN (*Vaguely amused.*): She'd do it . . .

KELLER (*To Sédaria.*): Everything considered, the legionnaires mustn't have had a very good time with you.

KAJIN: You're both blowing up at one another as if you wanted to sleep together.

SÉDARIA: Shut up! You're crazy.

KAJIN: Let's conclude. (*To Keller.*) Tomorrow morning, behind the bandstand, someone will give you a package.

KELLER: How will I recognize this someone?

KAJIN: He will recognize you.

KELLER: Ah! And the bomb, to make it work?

KAJIN: The instructions will be written on the wrapping. Five o'clock sharp. That's the time the proceedings officially begin at the military tribunal. Keep that in mind. Four of our people in front of judges who have made up their minds beforehand!

KELLER: Justice by class. Maybe I will be thinking of them at H hour! Perhaps I'll have other worries.

KAJIN: Keep your eyes open and everything will go all right.

KELLER: Let's hope so.

KAJIN: We're leaving first. See you tomorrow.

Kajin, going by, gives Keller a friendly tap on the shoulder. Then he pushes Sédaria ahead of him. They disappear rapidly while Keller, remaining alone, suddenly seems overwhelmed.

SCENE 3

Hazelhoff, Schultz, Keller. The light returns as in Scene 1.

HAZELHOFF (*To Keller who hasn't changed place.*): You are clever. You only tell us what we already know. All right. But a night spent thinking it all over didn't bring you around to a wholesome view of things?

KELLER: Yes, all that night I thought about what I was going to do. And in spite of myself I always came back to those four comrades who would be shot because they were right.

SCHULTZ: Mrs. Keller would be curious to learn it was the fate of these very four bandits that caused your insomnia that night.

KELLER: Oh, I thought about her too. But since she had chosen to go away, to leave me . . .

SCHULTZ: In brief, you said to yourself that on board the *Breda*, despite the power station duly sabotaged, she wouldn't suffer from the lack of an electric fan or refrigerator.

HAZELHOFF: What frightens me about you, Keller, is that you were already ready to betray all the moral values our country is defending here.

KELLER: Was it in the name of these moral values, for instance, that they raped Sédaria?

HAZELHOFF: Would you deny we brought progress here? We built. We have healed, educated. Obviously there have been mistakes. But our balance sheet is for the most part positive.

KELLER: The planters build shacks for their personnel just as European peasants build stables for their horses. They all say: look how well housed they are. The progress you talk about isn't enough to give a man his dignity; maybe it's just the contrary.

HAZELHOFF: Come now, Keller! We still have a great mission to accomplish in this part of the world where history has placed us. A mission worthy of our traditions, of our creative genius. If we left, there would be chaos! Do we have the right to allow millions of people to go to their ruin?

KELLER: The majority of Europeans who come into this country think first of making a lot of money exploiting the natives. Even at the plant the salaries of the Indonesian workers, for equal work, are lower than ours.

SCHULTZ: I congratulate you for thinking so generously of your fellow workers. May I remind you, however, that the day before yesterday you were still quite close to blowing their insides out!

KELLER: That's not true!

SCHULTZ: What? You didn't bring that device into the power station? You didn't place it exactly in the spot agreed on?

HAZELHOFF: Come, let's go over this business from the beginning. So you go into the hydroelectric station without awakening the guard's suspicions. The bomb was hidden in newspaper inside a shopping bag. You keep it until the favorable moment. Isn't that it?

KELLER: Yes.

HAZELHOFF: The moment arrived. What time was it?

KELLER: Three o'clock.

HAZELHOFF: No difficulties in carrying out the operation?

KELLER: The room was deserted.

HAZELHOFF: No one saw you and you activated the bomb.

KELLER: I hid behind a pillar.

SCHULTZ: Three o'clock, you say? But the foreman caught you much later!

KELLER: It's just that things became complicated.

HAZELHOFF: At three o'clock, your operations terminated, you returned to your shop. Is that it?

KELLER: Yes. And I kept watch from my place. I was nervous. Especially when I saw two native workers go into the room to clean up.

SCHULTZ: And you were afraid for your bomb?

KELLER: No, for them.

SCHULTZ: Come on now!

KELLER: I wanted to think of a pretext to get them out of there, but I couldn't think of anything and time was going by. The hour was getting near and they were still there. One of them was even singing. Then I made up my mind.

SCHULTZ: Made up your mind to do what?

KELLER: I went back into the room and defused the bomb.

Silence.

HAZELHOFF: When did they catch you?

KELLER: When I was crossing the courtyard. It was then I met the foreman. He looked at me in a certain way and I thought I'd be a gonner if I continued on my way. But I still heard the other fool singing over there.

HAZELHOFF: And you went and defused the bomb just the same.

KELLER: Eh! I just couldn't . . .

Vague gesture.

HAZELHOFF: On your way back you were arrested and taken back to the head office.

KELLER: Yes.

SCHULTZ: And the foreman struck you first!

Silence.

HAZELHOFF: Your statements coincide rather closely with what we know. Is that all? Nothing more to say?

KELLER: As a matter of fact . . .

SCHULTZ: What?

KELLER: To make the two lookouts talk, you certainly must have . . . They informed you too well!

SCHULTZ (*Curtly.*): What is essential is, they informed us.

KELLER: You admit, then, they were tortured!

SCHULTZ: Keller, you're the accused!

KELLER: Will you be surprised afterwards if their relatives try to avenge them?

HAZELHOFF: That's enough. We will continue in a little while. We will still have other questions to ask you and you will sign your statements.

He rings. A policeman enters. Keller joins him, leaves first, followed by the recording clerk.

SCENE 4

Hazelhoff, Schultz.

SCHULTZ: That story about a defused bomb, has it been proved?

HAZELHOFF: Absolutely. That's the surprise I had in store for you. Look at the ordnance people's report.

SCHULTZ: The change of heart won't save him.

HAZELHOFF: Is that a wish?

SCHULTZ: A conviction.

HAZELHOFF: There is a fellow who can still feel pity. In times like ours, you must agree yourself, it's not very common.

SCHULTZ: However, you still have to hold against him the fact that, in spite of everything, he collaborates with our enemies and supports their cause unconditionally. The pity you talk about was perhaps only a lapse caused by the magnitude of the project. A healthy fear brought about by more clearly perceived consequences!

HAZELHOFF: Even seen that way, isn't it all to his advantage?

SCHULTZ: You are making a premature judgment, it seems to me.

HAZELHOFF (*Smiling.*): Schultz, I think you are telling me that you take me for a tenderhearted old fogey.

SCHULTZ: I don't think that at all.

HAZELHOFF: Come on, I distinctly noticed the tone you used in repeating the word "pity." But look at the facts again. By leaving the bomb in place, Keller would not necessarily have been suspected. Moreover, how could anything have been proved against him? The plant employs a lot of people. But he retraced his steps to save the lives of two poor coolies and, for having changed his mind, he gave himself away.

SCHULTZ: We are only preparing the case. Others will judge it.

HAZELHOFF: Yes. And there is Kajin and that girl who worry me. At liberty they are more dangerous than a thousand cobras set loose in the city.

SCHULTZ: We will have to take a firmer hand with Keller concerning his two accomplices.

HAZELHOFF (*Rather bitter.*): Inspector Rijn has already taken care of the two lookouts with a very firm hand, Schultz, extremely firm, I believe . . .

SCHULTZ: This Keller isn't at all the way I thought he would be. He makes demands, he objects, he accuses. That indicates character, an inner strength.

HAZELHOFF: In truth, the touchy point is that our man refused to kill. If he had killed, nothing more ordinary. How easy for everyone! With that said, Schultz, do me a favor. Let them know at home that I won't come for lunch. I have work. They are clamoring for the Keller file as soon as possible. This story has stirred up enormous commotion in all circles!

SCHULTZ: I'll phone Mrs. Hazelhoff, count on me, sir. Don't you want at least a sandwich?

HAZELHOFF: No, thank you. The drugs Dr. Van Rook gives me upset my stomach. See you later.

SCHULTZ: Yes, sir.

He exits. Remaining alone, Hazelhoff begins to write. He puts one hand on his side as if suffering a shooting pain. Then he lets himself fall back wearily at the

CURTAIN

ACT THREE

SCENE 1

As the curtain goes up the stage is empty. A shade hides the bay window facing the garden. Hazelhoff comes in. He takes off his panama hat wearily and goes to raise the shade. The full light of the tropical morning penetrates into the room. At this moment the telephone rings.

HAZELHOFF: Hello? The Attorney General? Yes, certainly, connect me with him. Hello? Good day, Your Honor. Yes, I was indisposed during the night. Oh, neither better nor worse. Doctor Van Rook . . . I had him called. Thank you, Your Honor . . . We interrogated Keller the whole day. His file will be ready this afternoon. Schultz is putting it in final shape. Yes, not the slightest doubt. The ordnance report is explicit and no one has been able to come close to the bomb since the moment of Keller's arrest. That's right. We shall have finished with him by tonight. Then he will be transferred to Fort Soeliko. Yes, Your Honor. Thank you.

He hangs up. Schultz has come in during his last words.

SCENE 2

Hazelhoff, Schultz.

SCHULTZ: Hello, sir.

HAZELHOFF: Hello, Schultz. (*He points to the telephone.*) That was the

Attorney General. He would like to have the file as soon as possible. His impatience bothers me.

SCHULTZ: I will do my best to help you.

HAZELHOFF: Thanks, but this impatience bothers me especially the way it reveals public unrest over the Keller affair. I don't like quick justice.

SCHULTZ: Did you notice the tone of this morning's newspapers?

He points out the newspapers laid out on Hazelhoff's table.

HAZELHOFF: There are sensational headlines for you! They were perhaps in too much of a hurry to divulge the news.

SCHULTZ: Oh, it was already going about town, sir, and had even gone beyond.

HAZELHOFF: I know, I know . . . Van Rook informed me.

SCHULTZ: You must have had to call Dr. Van Rook?

HAZELHOFF: In the middle of the night. An unbearable attack! I had worked late and just as I was going to bed, zip! Stabbed!

SCHULTZ: I am terribly sorry for you, sir.

HAZELHOFF: Mind you, Van Rook didn't take long. Five minutes after my call, he made a buffoon's entrance at my place!

SCHULTZ: Was he able to give you some relief?

HAZELHOFF: Yes, but what was no less interesting was that he jabbered on as usual. You have to listen to Van Rook. He sees people every day. And they say a lot of things about Keller.

SCHULTZ: Really? For instance?

HAZELHOFF: Just listen . . . It must have been past midnight.

Schultz has stepped back. The lights go out. Hazelhoff alone remains illuminated, seated at his table and his hand to his side. Van Rook enters through the moonlit French door.

SCENE 3

Hazelhoff, Van Rook, and Schultz in the background in the dark as if listening to the narration of the scene.

VAN ROOK: Is this for a death certificate?

HAZELHOFF: Thank you for your haste, doctor.

VAN ROOK: You had the voice of a dying man on the other end of the line. What about your wife? She could have taken the trouble to come.

HAZELHOFF: I didn't want her to be alarmed.

VAN ROOK (*While emptying his bag.*): Come now! Women like that. Taking care of a sick husband, especially if he is very sick, is the crowning point of their career as a spouse. According to very serious studies, they are prepared for widowhood just as they are for motherhood.

HAZELHOFF: Ah? Just as for motherhood?

VAN ROOK: I would have arrived sooner if a patrol hadn't thought it a good idea to check my permit to move about after blackout time. I said: "Hurry up! A magistrate is dying!"

HAZELHOFF (*Modest.*): Oh, dying!

VAN ROOK: And do you know what the sergeant answered? "A judge? Let him croak!"

HAZELHOFF: Still another who probably thinks our profession is useless in this country.

VAN ROOK: Come this way a little. It hurts you here, is that right?

HAZELHOFF (*Resigned.*): Yes.

VAN ROOK: I already advised you to return to Europe. But you are only an obstinate . . . And there?

HAZELHOFF: There too.

VAN ROOK: You also felt some pains like knife jabs, isn't that right?

HAZELHOFF: The whole day. And not like a knife stabbing but like a red-hot sabre ably manipulated by a Chinese executioner! Are you satisfied?

VAN ROOK (*With relish.*): Don't talk nonsense! You are done for, Hazelhoff. Done for! Do you hear me? You have a slight chance if you leave here, but very slight.

HAZELHOFF: Then what's the use, Van Rook?

VAN ROOK: That's your concern. Anyway, I am going to prescribe a drug that will give you relief.

HAZELHOFF: Let's not lose a minute.

VAN ROOK (*Jubilant.*): I didn't say "that will cure you."

HAZELHOFF: I was able to make the distinction without any help.

Van Rook has taken a pharmaceutical case from his bag. He fills a glass with water in which he dilutes the contents of an ampule, and so forth. While this little operation is going on, the dialogue continues.

HAZELHOFF: Let's speak clearly. How much time do I still have?

VAN ROOK (*Disdainfully.*): Pff . . .

HAZELHOFF (*Ironically.*): So little?

VAN ROOK: How am I supposed to know? If you leave, three or four years, I think. In Holland you would have a healthful climate, creamy milk, pastures . . .

HAZELHOFF: Pastures? Really, what do you expect me to do with them? Am I supposed to graze? And . . . if I remain?

VAN ROOK: A year . . . Eighteen months, perhaps, by taking quite a lot of this filthy stuff . . .

HAZELHOFF: Does it have a good taste?

VAN ROOK: I warn you that taken in big doses it will produce disagreeable effects, loss of memory, anxiety, hallucinations.

HAZELHOFF: You reassure me.

VAN ROOK: Something important keeping you here?

HAZELHOFF: Nothing important attracting me back there. Besides, here or back there, isn't it always the appointment at Samarkand?

VAN ROOK: What wisdom! I see that the Asia that has rotted your body has nourished your mind.

HAZELHOFF: Van Rook, I heard your voice stating how much time I have left. It had the indifference and remoteness of those sentences that fall on mortals from heaven. Ah, what a fine actor you would have made!

VAN ROOK: It's just that you judges deserve the most dreadful death.

HAZELHOFF (*Smiling.*): Why, for God's sake?

VAN ROOK: For having inflicted it yourselves on other men!

HAZELHOFF: In the name of Society, Van Rook!

VAN ROOK: I am opposed to tribunals based on violence. Society can simply use other means to defend itself!

HAZELHOFF: But, Van Rook . . .

VAN ROOK: Drink that.

HAZELHOFF (*Drinks*.): Thanks.

VAN ROOK: I will come back to see you tomorrow. Keep the box. Two ampules a day. Complete rest all week.

HAZELHOFF: Impossible. I have important and urgent work to conclude.

VAN ROOK: As you wish . . .

He puts the glass back in place and begins to fold up his case.

HAZELHOFF: I am preparing the Keller case, you know.

VAN ROOK: Still another who would have done better not to get involved.

HAZELHOFF: What are they saying about him, Van Rook? I would like to know.

VAN ROOK: I know a doctor who sometimes goes into the dissident area to take care of the peasants.

HAZELHOFF: He treats them for nothing and also furnishes them free medicine. The natives adore him and swear only by him.

VAN ROOK: Which proves at least that they are capable of loving someone who loves them!

HAZELHOFF: This doctor, however, runs the risk of getting himself killed by a too nervous sentinel or of being captured by a patrol.

VAN ROOK: Oh, he takes his precautions.

HAZELHOFF: If just one of his precautions fails, these little jaunts among the rebels can cost him five to ten years in prison.

VAN ROOK: I know, I know.

HAZELHOFF: I see we are talking about the same individual.

VAN ROOK: In the dissident areas they knew about the Keller affair almost immediately.

HAZELHOFF: What were the commentaries?

VAN ROOK: Rather varied. They are awaiting the court's decision with curiosity. Last month didn't this same tribunal condemn young Sadravi to death?

HAZELHOFF: Sadravi? A grenade in a movie theatre!

VAN ROOK: But it didn't explode.

HAZELHOFF: That wasn't his fault.

VAN ROOK: It doesn't matter. There weren't any victims. They shot him just the same. A child. Seventeen years old. An only son!

HAZELHOFF: What! He admitted the facts and was sorry the grenade didn't explode.

VAN ROOK: He was a kid.

HAZELHOFF: I understand. The natives are waiting for the judges to show the same harshness toward a man of their own race.

VAN ROOK: Not exactly. The common people were moved to learn a European worker had espoused their cause, and especially that he balked at the idea of assassinating two anonymous coolies. They are not much used to finding among us that kind of feeling toward them.

HAZELHOFF: Yet for certain hotheads, if one of our compatriots has joined the rebel cause, he ought to incur the risks as those not having the same skin color; is that it?

VAN ROOK: Only for certain hotheads, as you put it . . . And probably because in this country there have been two kinds of justice for too long.

HAZELHOFF: And it will be difficult to make anyone agree that Keller deserves extenuating circumstances since it has actually been proved he refused to kill!

VAN ROOK: Even if Keller had killed, as far as I am concerned, I would refuse to have him killed in his turn.

HAZELHOFF: I know, I know. Gandhi, always Gandhi, isn't it?

VAN ROOK: Of course, Gandhi! Just listen to him . . . (*His tone of voice changes.*) "A few days ago a young student tried to assassinate me. I only ask one thing: may God protect him . . ."

HAZELHOFF: Ah, how you love noble souls!

VAN ROOK: Don't be ironic, good judge! Listen to what follows. (*Same tone*.) "At all times my philosophy has set my line of conduct, which has been that of a man devoted to total pacifism! In spite of the recent events that have just shaken the world and that still stir it, I, Gandhi, do not believe in violence, for in this world there exists an immanent justice that sooner or later will bear fruit!"

HAZELHOFF: Gandhi's last message before his death eight months ago!

VAN ROOK: And no one can deny that India gained its independence thanks to Gandhi's theories. Even the last English governor admitted it.

HAZELHOFF: Note that the Indian people paid dearly for their independence in prisons and camps.

VAN ROOK: No more dearly than if they had fought with a weapon in their hands trading blow for blow with their adversaries. An unblemished victory without an assassination, Hazelhoff! Think about it and stop trying to pull my leg.

HAZELHOFF: But doctor! What I find amusing is that you were trying to convince me when it would be better to preach these truths among your friends in the hills!

VAN ROOK: Oh, I say it to them enough. No cause in the world is worth killing for it. But I am thinking of Keller. In spite of everything, I admire the fact that he followed instinctively, by a natural inclination of his heart, a precept he didn't even know. In that he seems to me infinitely superior to the Pope.

HAZELHOFF: The Pope? What is the Pope doing in this, Van Rook?

VAN ROOK: What?—the sixth commandment didn't prevent him from approving of a certain war nor from blessing the cannons. Good night, old judge! See you tomorrow.

HAZELHOFF: Good night, doctor.

SCENE 4

Hazelhoff, Schultz. Daylight has returned. It finds Hazelhoff in the exact place Schultz left him.

HAZELHOFF: Imagine yourself in the dissident zone, busy talking about total pacifism and passive resistance to guerrillas covered with cartridge belts and armed to the teeth.

SCHULTZ: You ought to follow his advice, sir, and leave for Europe. Back there you could recover your health.

HAZELHOFF: Oh, recover my health!

SCHULTZ: I sincerely hope so, sir.

HAZELHOFF: Thank you for your good thoughts, Schultz. But we are still supposed to hear Keller. *(He glances at a newspaper.)* If his trial were to take place anywhere else but this city, I would give him a little better chance. But here in this poisoned atmosphere . . .

The telephone rings. Schultz grabs it.

SCHULTZ: Yes. One minute . . . *(To Hazelhoff.)* Mr. Van Ooster is asking to see you.

HAZELHOFF: Right away?

SCHULTZ: Yes, sir. He is in the waiting room.

HAZELHOFF *(Sullen.)*: He certainly picks his time! See if he can come back in the afternoon. Diplomatically, all right?

SCHULTZ *(Uncovering the phone.)*: Hello? Mr. Hazelhoff is busy. Couldn't you . . . Ah . . . I understand . . . It's important. *(To the judge.)* He insists, sir . . .

HAZELHOFF *(Irritated.)*: All right. Tell him to come in.

SCHULTZ *(Into the phone.)*: In that case, sir, he is waiting for you.

He hangs up.

HAZELHOFF *(In a bad mood.)*: These big planters like to play the great chiefs. Everything seems to belong to them. All doors are open to them. They do . . . *(Van Ooster comes in. Hazelhoff immediately adopts an amiable tone of voice which, being a little forced, makes the irony perceptible.)* How are you my dear friend? What a pleasure to welcome you! Please do have a seat.

Van Ooster had already sat down.

VAN OOSTER *(Stern.)*: Hazelhoff, you look wonderful!

HAZELHOFF: Really?

VAN OOSTER *(Who doesn't give a rap.)*: Really!

HAZELHOFF: Not to hide anything from you, Dr. Van Rook contemplates burying me at the end of the year.

VAN OOSTER: Dr. Van Rook has always had a dark sense of humour.

HAZELHOFF: That's reassuring.

VAN OOSTER: I swear you have a better complexion than you did about two weeks ago.

HAZELHOFF: That's perhaps due to my new shaving cream.

VAN OOSTER: Don't listen to Van Rook. And drink scotch. Only scotch. But a lot of scotch!

HAZELHOFF: I'll see to it.

VAN OOSTER: At any rate, two weeks ago you had an awful complexion. At the time I said to myself: the good judge is not long for this world. But I see that everything has taken care of itself.

HAZELHOFF: Thanks for the encouragement. But to what do I owe the pleasure of this morning visit?

VAN OOSTER (*Gets up.*): A very serious affair.

HAZELHOFF: I am listening.

VAN OOSTER: You are preparing the Keller case and a rumor is going about town that alarms us.

HAZELHOFF: Who is "us"?

VAN OOSTER: We, the Europeans. The planters.

HAZELHOFF: Explain yourself.

VAN OOSTER: We've been told a preposterous story about a deactivated timing mechanism, a defused bomb, an explosion averted, I don't know what all. It's our guess that it's all a maneuver to try to save the neck of this Keller, who, in spite of everything, remains a fellow countryman. Well, we protest against this maneuver. And we are ready to denounce it.

HAZELHOFF: Van Ooster, you have known me for twenty-five or thirty years.

VAN OOSTER: Yes.

HAZELHOFF: And so much time hasn't been enough to convince you that I am not a man to consent to what you call a maneuver?

VAN OOSTER: Just a moment! You mean it's true, that in Keller's . . .

HAZELHOFF: It's true, it has been proved that Keller, affected by scruples at the last moment, refused to sacrifice two individuals who were working in the room and would have been pulverized by the explosion.

VAN OOSTER: How do you mean, proved?

HAZELHOFF: Absolute proof!

VAN OOSTER: Let's talk seriously, Hazelhoff. You understand what the feeling of the European population was on learning one of their own had agreed to such a monstrous attempt! Indignation . . . would be putting it mildly.

HAZELHOFF: I suspect so.

VAN OOSTER: You understand, up to now we've only had to deal with native terrorists. Every European family knew the danger could only come from men of color. But if whites also become involved, then we will no longer be sure of anything. The danger becomes more serious, protection more difficult. It is appropriate then to show ourselves tougher, more ruthless toward a European who, like Keller, turns against his own.

HAZELHOFF: His own? You are the ones who are appropriating him. As far as he is concerned, he has chosen. His own are in the opposite camp. He is one of us only by the color of his skin and he thinks that insufficient.

VAN OOSTER: In a word, a real traitor! And if he backed off it was because he was afraid.

HAZELHOFF: On the contrary, if blood hadn't made him balk, he'd have been safe. But he belongs to our damnable times in which it is often necessary to sacrifice some men to save others. He had a doubt and so he was caught.

VAN OOSTER: Well, for us there is no doubt: he must be properly shot and within the shortest possible time.

HAZELHOFF: That's up to the court to judge, Van Ooster!

VAN OOSTER: The court, the court! Do we need all that ceremony for rabble like Keller? If it were up to us, believe me . . .

HAZELHOFF: I believe you.

VAN OOSTER: Sentencing him to a prison term, even a long one, is out of the question! Twelve bullets! We demand it! We need an example. We must prevent any repetition, discourage any new Kellers.

HAZELHOFF: Justice is unconcerned with the desire for vengeance, Van Ooster. It is unruffled and equal for all.

VAN OOSTER: It is, above all, slow. Terribly slow!

HAZELHOFF: Enough time is needed, at least, to examine the case conscientiously. A human life is important.

VAN OOSTER: Go tell that to Keller's friends.

HAZELHOFF: Gladly, if the occasion occurs.

VAN OOSTER: We must show ourselves much more relentless. Our enemies must feel and fear our determination. Let them know we are without mercy. Strike hard! Frighten them until they fall to their knees.

HAZELHOFF: What's that! The language of a terrorist!

VAN OOSTER: I'm not joking!

HAZELHOFF: Nor am I! (*A silence. Van Ooster wipes his lips.*) In brief, you came to see me for fear that a given good intention on the part of the guilty person might serve to save him from the worst. Now, well, you see Keller has refused for other people what you wish for him!

VAN OOSTER: No more of your clever dodges, Hazelhoff. Keller has to be the first and last white man to have dared!

HAZELHOFF: I would like to know if you can imagine this man who refused to kill awaiting his own death in a casemate at Fort Soeliko. I would like to know if you can imagine the last night and the last morning? You have never seen an execution by bullets? The volley makes a hole in the chest you could put your fist through.

VAN OOSTER (*Violently.*): You won't get me with that kind of description, Hazelhoff! Yesterday I went to the hospital where they were treating the wounded from the market. Do you want me in my turn to describe to you the stumps of the little girl who had both her feet torn off? And the explosion, you know, killed a young woman who was pregnant. She had her belly opened and her entrails were lying on the ground along with what should have become a baby! Do you want me to continue, Hazelhoff? Do you want me to?

HAZELHOFF: Van Ooster, the young man whose death you are demanding recoiled before precisely the horrors you are talking about.

VAN OOSTER: What does that matter! He betrayed us. That's all that counts.

HAZELHOFF: As far as I am concerned, I only prepare the case. What follows falls within the competence of the court.

VAN OOSTER: It's a good thing it's a military court!

HAZELHOFF: Why?

VAN OOSTER: You can hope for a little more from military judges who know the kind of vile treatment our soldiers undergo in the hands of the guerrillas.

HAZELHOFF: Military judges are also judges!

VAN OOSTER: Do you know what the rebels did to the three young soldiers they captured Monday? They emasculated them, then tied them up facing the sun with bamboo needles under their eyelids.

HAZELHOFF: Come, Van Ooster, calm down! And please have faith in justice.

VAN OOSTER (*Beside himself.*): Have faith! You are talking a little bit soon, my friend. You, you are a civil servant. And this war is not completely yours, isn't that so? When your time is finished you'll leave again for Europe. But for us what's at stake here goes far beyond the life of this Keller. He spared the lives of two coolies, you say. Isn't that fine! But we're the ones you ought to have faith in. We're going to take good care of him. You can rest assured on that point!

He leaves at a brisk pace without saying good-bye or turning around.

SCENE 5

Hazelhoff, Schultz.

HAZELHOFF: A real hurricane!

SCHULTZ: What could he possibly do? What do his threats mean?

HAZELHOFF: Oh, he is powerful! And he is defending enormous interests in this country! As a matter of fact, compared to the present market price of petroleum and crude rubber, the life of an overly sensitive electrical worker may seem ridiculously cheap.

SCHULTZ: The planters are fighting with their backs to the sea, sir.

HAZELHOFF: Facing them, the others fight with their backs to poverty. There is despair and hatred on both sides. That's what makes this war so cruel.

The telephone rings.

SCHULTZ (*On the phone.*): What's that you say, sergeant? Hello? Wait. (*To Hazelhoff.*) Mrs. Keller has just arrived, sir.

HAZELHOFF: Let her come in, let her come in. I authorized her to see her husband. Tell them what to do concerning Keller as well. I insist this meeting take place right here.

SCHULTZ (*On the phone.*): Ask the lady to come in and go get Keller in the infirmary.

He hangs up.

SCENE 6

The same personages plus Kitty.

KITTY: Hello, gentlemen.

HAZELHOFF (*Cursorily.*): My respects, Madam. Your husband will be here in a minute. According to regulations your visit cannot exceed a few minutes and you are not permitted to speak in a low voice.

KITTY: Yes, sir. The judgment is for tomorrow afternoon, isn't it?

HAZELHOFF: Theoretically, yes.

KITTY: And my husband's life is threatened.

HAZELHOFF: Nothing is lost yet.

KITTY: Will I be able to see him again tomorrow morning before he is transferred to Soeliko?

HAZELHOFF: Granted. Five minutes. The same time.

KITTY: Thank you.

HAZELHOFF: Here is Keller. I will leave you.

Before leaving he makes a little gesture to Schultz as if to say: "Keep your eyes open."

SCENE 7

Schultz, Kitty, then Keller who enters through the other door accompanied by policemen.

KITTY (*Moved.*): Johann . . .

KELLER: Ah, it's true the *Breda* is supposed to sail at noon.

KITTY: You're crazy, Johann! Don't talk like that.

KELLER: I hope you are going to go on board and leave.

KITTY: You don't mean it!

KELLER: All right. Do as you wish. You are free, after all.

KITTY: Why such an attitude, Johann, at a moment like this!

KELLER: At a moment like this I perhaps need to be alone.

KITTY: You seem to want to get even with me.

KELLER: It's simpler than that. I would prefer to know you were on the *Breda*, to know you were safe, away from all this. You are very poorly prepared for this kind of adventure.

KITTY: I dreaded it but I was prepared for it!

KELLER: So that's it!

KITTY: You must agree to see your lawyer.

KELLER: I finally agreed.

KITTY (*In a softer, more animated voice.*): You saw him?

KELLER (*Same as before.*): This morning. He is encouraging me to state I acted under duress.

KITTY (*Same as before.*): Follow his advice. Say they threatened to kill you if you didn't obey!

KELLER: Come now! I volunteered. I admitted it in this very room.

KITTY: You can retract it! You can always retract.

KELLER: I refuse to play the farce of a man who acted under the effects of fear.

KITTY: But it's a necessary lie! A lie that could save you!

KELLER: No. That would be the same as renouncing everything. And if it hadn't been for those two poor devils, I swear I was determined to go all the way! Sabotage, I accept. Sabotage is a weapon of revolution.

KITTY: Once more, Johann, if you don't lie they are going to give you a harsh sentence. You're taking a big risk!

SCHULTZ (*Energetically.*): Conversations in a low voice are prohibited! If you continue, I'll have to put an end to the visit.

A silence.

KELLER (*Now in a normal voice.*): I refuse to claim I gave in to a threat. I acted out of conviction and I'll hold to it!

KITTY (*Also in a normal voice.*): Still you have to help your lawyer defend you. You must assemble as many as possible arguments in your favor.

KELLER: I will defend myself without cheating. I insist on being judged exactly for what I am and on what I have done.

KITTY: Without renouncing anything—as you say—you can still avoid being too outspoken, Johann. Your defense has to be worked out carefully.

KELLER: It will be.

KITTY: If you speak in a provocative manner you will turn your judges against you.

KELLER: I won't be provocative but I won't consent to certain clever dodges, either.

KITTY: Be careful, Johann! (*She says these words glancing furtively toward Schultz who, reading some documents, is seated in front of his desk. She becomes bold and reverts to a low tone, very quickly.*) A man came to the house early this morning. He suggested I meet a person you know.

KELLER (*Same tone.*): Who, then?

KITTY: He didn't tell me his name.

KELLER: Watch out. It might be a police trick.

KITTY: I don't think so.

KELLER: You agreed?

KITTY: Yes. He will come back to get me tonight before curfew.

KELLER: If it's not a police maneuver, then my comrades sent him. And if they are anxious to see you, they are concerned about me. What are you going to tell them?

KITTY: It's they who want to speak to me.

KELLER: How can I find out what they wanted?

KITTY: I'll come back here tomorrow morning. The judge has agreed to it.

KELLER (*Same as before but with more emphasis.*): Tell the comrades I would have agreed to be killed myself but I couldn't for the two others. Tell them they mustn't hold it against me.

SCHULTZ (*Gets up with cold animosity.*): I warned you! You are beginning again! Madam, I am sorry . . . It's over.

He motions to the guards. They take away Keller who can just barely wave to his wife before disappearing.

SCENE 8

Schultz, Kitty.

SCHULTZ: You both caused me to apply the regulation strictly.

KITTY: I fully understand, sir.

SCHULTZ: I heard, however, the sound advice you were giving your husband. It's true his file appears quite heavy!

KITTY (*Mordantly.*): In many ways it would appear very light if compared to the files of certain rich planters of the region!

She goes toward the door and leaves. Schultz shrugs his shoulders and returns to his table at the

CURTAIN

ACT FOUR

SCENE 1

Schultz, then the Guard. Policemen. As the curtain goes up Schultz is on the threshold. It's the morning after that of the third act. The telephone rings.

SCHULTZ: Yes! (*With irritation.*) Of course not! No newspaper people! I don't give a damn! You can answer anything you wish.

He hangs up violently. A knock at the door. Schultz shouts "Come in." The Guard enters surrounded by police.

SCHULTZ (*In a bad mood.*): There you are! You are leaving for Soeliko. Admit you had the six months coming! (*The telephone rings again. Schultz, irritated, grabs it.*) Yes, speaking . . . Mr. Hazelhoff was indisposed again last night. I don't know. Perhaps in an hour, perhaps later. I can't tell you anything! Sorry, sir! (*He hangs up sharply. Then to the Guard.*) You are getting off easy!

GUARD (*Pitiably.*): The lawyer, however, clearly explained that the Europeans refused to let themselves be searched.

SCHULTZ (*Disgusted.*): Result: six months at Soeliko. But cheer up: they are going to put you up in the part where the buildings have been renovated and you won't be with the natives. Here, sign here.

GUARD: Ah, thank you very much.

He signs.

SCHULTZ: And if you don't cause any trouble, perhaps you will obtain a reduction of your sentence.

GUARD: Thank you again, sir. I will try to behave well and get a good rating.

SCHULTZ: Don't thank me so much. If it had been up to me, I would have sent you to the Jakarta prison. I swear the six months would appear much longer over there.

GUARD: You have it in for me!

The telephone rings. Schultz, furious, on the phone: "Don't let anyone disturb me! I am busy! Until further notice, have all calls handled by the secretarial staff!" He hangs up, exasperated.

SCHULTZ: But you yourself must have it in for Keller for putting you in this mess.

GUARD: Oh, Keller could have let the bomb explode. And, who knows, if he had refused to plant the bomb, the others might have managed to do it themselves. In that case, then, there would have been the devil to pay!

SCHULTZ (*With malicious irony.*): So in your opinion it's lucky Keller accepted? Is that it?

GUARD (*Disturbed.*): To a certain extent, sir . . .

SCHULTZ: You are even a bigger fool than I supposed. Go on.

He motions to the policemen who take the man away.

SCENE 2

The instant the guard leaves on the right, Hazelhoff enters from the rear. He takes off his Panama hat and mops his face.

SCHULTZ: Good day, sir.

HAZELHOFF: Hello, Schultz. Really I can't go the fifty yards from the taxi to this room any more without being exhausted.

SCHULTZ: Did you have pain again last night?

HAZELHOFF: Quite an attack. But this time Van Rook gave me an injection of I don't know what special formula of his that really gave me relief. It wasn't Gandhi who was talked about this time but Rondon.

SCHULTZ: Rondon? Who is that?

HAZELHOFF: Another of the people Van Rook admires. He is the Brazilian who pacified the Indians in the Amazon forest by following the principle: "Let yourself be killed rather than kill!" A veritable saint!

SCHULTZ: Saints and heroes, it's all a question of diet. Have you noticed great saints are generally vegetarians and heroes eat too much red meat?

HAZELHOFF: It's a point of view. All right. Let's get to work.

SCHULTZ: The telephone hasn't stopped ringing. I silenced it to breathe a little. Have you read the newspapers, sir? Last night's demonstration was really impressive.

HAZELHOFF: Van Ooster, it's obvious! If the demonstrators had been able to find their way to Keller, they would simply have lynched him. What's that?

Schultz hands him a paper.

SCHULTZ: An order from the Governor to transfer Keller this very morning to Soeliko under a heavy escort.

HAZELHOFF: I see. They are afraid of a new flare-up. But why the devil did our compatriots break into and destroy the native stores!

SCHULTZ: Their nerves are shattered.

HAZELHOFF: A beautiful pretext, Schultz! The police should have been able to hold them back. (*Hazelhoff sits down.*) And our young female prisoner? Where are we with her? Did she seem less violent to you this morning?

SCHULTZ: Just as full of poison as yesterday, sir.

HAZELHOFF: She is very pretty.

SCHULTZ: An authentic killer. She's not afraid of death whether it's a question of killing or being killed.

HAZELHOFF: And that?

He points to a packet of letters.

SCHULTZ: Anonymous letters the Governor turned over to us. People demanding Keller's immediate execution.

HAZELHOFF: Bah. (*He wearily looks over a few letters.*) And this girl admitted the facts?

SCHULTZ: See the report, sir . . .

HAZELHOFF (*Takes the papers.*): Well, she claims all responsibility. She would begin again if she had the opportunity. What hatred!

SCHULTZ: When I informed the Governor this morning of her capture, I had a hard time convincing him to keep the secret until at least tomorrow.

HAZELHOFF: He wanted to blare it out right away to prove the efficiency of his administration.

SCHULTZ: We have to arrange a confrontation between this girl and Keller to complete the file.

HAZELHOFF: It's a formality but necessary. It's good that it will only be after Mrs. Keller's visit. I saw her in the waiting room. Arrange an immediate meeting with her husband and get that over with.

SCHULTZ: I'll give the orders, sir.

He leaves.

SCENE 3

Hazelhoff remains alone an instant leafing gloomily through the report. Kitty enters from the rear. Then Keller, on the right, with policemen.

HAZELHOFF: Good day, Madam . . . (*She seems tired and he notices it.*) Once more, I can only allow you a few minutes . . .

KITTY: I am grateful for them.

HAZELHOFF: But for this occasion I am going to authorize you to be alone.

KITTY: Thank you, sir.

HAZELHOFF: I suppose you won't give me cause to regret it.

Keller shakes his head. Hazelhoff motions to the policemen who leave to the right. Hazelhoff follows them.

SCENE 4

Keller, Kitty.

KELLER: He's leaving us alone because I'm departing in a little while for Soeliko. He thinks we won't see one another again.

KITTY: Oh, no. I have confidence!

KELLER: And that demonstration! I heard the shouting from up there.

KITTY: They're trying to influence the judges.

KELLER: It's true a man's death can serve to instill fear. But did you go to that meeting? Tell me about it quickly. Whom did you meet?

KITTY (*Embarrassed.*): It was less important than it had seemed.

KELLER: Come now! Look at me! You mean they came to get you and made you run risks for nothing?

KITTY (*Weary.*): It was about a piece of information.

KELLER: What kind of information? Speak up. Who asked you there? (*Lower.*) Kajin, wasn't it?

KITTY: Yes.

KELLER: Speak then. What did he want from you? He regrets having given me the mission, eh?

KITTY: He regrets it.

KELLER: I want to know!

KITTY: They came for me an hour before curfew. They took me to a native house. At first I remained alone.

The lights go out as in the three preceding acts. Keller is in the dark. Kitty is illuminated by a spotlight which sets her off. Through the open French door, against the night, Kajin enters.

SCENE 5

The same characters plus Kajin.

KAJIN: Don't be afraid.

KITTY: I'm not afraid.

KAJIN: You are Keller's wife.

KITTY: Yes.

KAJIN: . . . Kajin. You weren't followed. There's nothing suspicious . . . Put yourself at ease.

KITTY: I'll take your word.

KAJIN: Our comrades were on the lookout all along your route.

KITTY: An excellent organization. That's reassuring. (*A silence.*) Well, here I am.

KAJIN: Were you able to meet Keller at the judge's this morning?

KITTY: What do you want to know?

KAJIN: The day before yesterday one of our people was arrested. Arrested by surprise. A stroke of luck for the police during a raid.

KITTY: And what can I tell you about it?

KAJIN: Our comrade had forged documents. If she hasn't been brought before Keller for a confrontation, it means the authorities don't know whom they have really captured.

KITTY: To reveal those facts to me you must be counting on my being discreet!

KAJIN (*With unfeigned gentleness.*): We can see to it that anyone remains discreet.

KITTY: Keller hasn't been confronted with anyone. He certainly would have talked to me about it this morning.

KAJIN: Did he have the possibility of telling you?

KITTY: Yes. We were watched but we were able to exchange a few remarks in a low voice.

KAJIN: The confrontation could have taken place this afternoon. Now you are to see Keller again.

KITTY: How do you know that?

KAJIN: You asked the taxi to come get you for the same run tomorrow morning.

KITTY: Why would such a confrontation take place? What link could there be between this girl and my husband?

KAJIN: It exists and it doesn't serve any purpose for you to know any more about it. But you must warn Keller if we still have time. Under no circumstance is he to reveal the real identity of this comrade.

KITTY: You want my husband to protect one of yours? To make himself somewhat of an accomplice to whatever she has done? You haven't understood then that Keller is different from you?

KAJIN: We understand that. But that's not the question.

A silence.

KITTY: Was it you who gave him the bomb?

KAJIN: Yes.

KITTY: And he agreed right away?

KAJIN: Right away!

A silence.

KITTY: Now you hate him.

KAJIN: No. But after his failure, if he had returned among us . . .

KITTY: Well?

KAJIN (*Quickly.*): We would have condemned him.

KITTY (*Same as before.*): But why?

KAJIN (*Same as before.*): This mission was to be carried out. He was a volunteer.

KITTY (*Same as before.*): You would kill him, wouldn't you?

KAJIN (*Same as before.*): We would apply the military code of the Royal Dutch Army which allows the death penalty for this kind of lapse.

KITTY: It was a question of an act of sabotage! Why require a set time that risked killing people? Why demand victims! And do you think you could really intimidate the judges preparing to judge your comrades?

KAJIN: Our people would have approved of this action in spite of the price it cost! They are desperate from having seen their best sons shot or tortured.

KITTY: Why add to so many horrors?

KAJIN: Your people commit atrocities every day because they think that in the long run the masses will be afraid and turn away from us for good. They don't know they are obtaining the opposite result.

KITTY: But you? You kill also with the same cruelty!

KAJIN: We give blow for blow. Without ever hesitating! No people in the world has ever freed itself without paying the price in blood. That, Keller forgot!

KITTY (*Bitter.*): Tomorrow night his judges will refresh his memory.

KAJIN: Judges terrorize also but to defend a society rich with privileges of which they are the watchdogs!

KITTY: And you, you take yourselves for watchdogs of the people, even more relentless, more savage! But do you know exactly what you are? Murderers!

KAJIN: Yes, Mrs. Keller, we are murderers . . . And if we have to sink even lower to save our people, we'll do it. And if there exists another life and if we have to lose it like this one to save our people, we accept that. (*With still greater simplicity.*) I don't think you know what our misery is really like . . .

KITTY (*Unconvinced.*): What am I to tell Keller?

KAJIN: Warn him tomorrow morning not to fall into the usual police trap.

KITTY: What trap?

KAJIN: Before any confrontation the police assert they know the truth because the other one has revealed everything. They even throw out the few details they might know to further favor confusion.

KITTY: But if your comrade has really confessed?

KAJIN: Our comrade will never admit anything, even under torture. And it is probable she will be rather badly treated if they suspect her real identity.

KITTY (*Resigned.*): I will warn Keller! But I must presume, then, that you still believe in him?

KAJIN: Not so fast! Tomorrow morning when you leave from your meeting with Keller, a man selling fans will come up to you. Tell him what you have learned. (*He goes toward the door.*) I am going to leave first.

KITTY: Is someone now going to accompany me back?

KAJIN: The same guide is to take you to the entrance of the European city.

He was already in front of the door. He goes out quickly. Lights. Keller finds himself in front of Kitty who only had to turn toward him.

SCENE 6

Kitty, Keller.

KELLER: I have been confronted with no one.

KITTY: Do you know who it is?

KELLER: They advised you to be discreet.

KITTY: I know how to keep a secret.

KELLER: If I tell you nothing, it will be easier for you.

KITTY: If you refuse to help the police, they will hold it against you.

KELLER: What do you mean by helping the police?

KITTY: Johann, you will compromise your case if they find out you know this girl and want to protect her.

KELLER: What do you advise? That I give her away?

KITTY: That you not dispose the judges towards refusing you extenuating circumstances.

KELLER (*Ironically.*): Ah! I don't deserve them?

KITTY: You have always sought to destroy yourself, Johann, and to the end I will not have been able to do anything for you.

KELLER: There you are freed since I am at the end!

KITTY: On a day like this must we leave one another as enemies?

KELLER (*Touched.*): I would have liked you to be happy.

KITTY: I know. We'll overcome these hardships together. Think that at the end of this war amnesty will be granted.

KELLER: I will be thinking of you, Kitty.

KITTY: No! First of what I just told you.

KELLER: Of course . . .

The tone of voice exasperates Kitty.

KITTY: Don't say "of course" like that! Please understand! You are more threatened than you think! You have refused to be interrogated in front of your lawyer. But if you don't help him more tonight, you are risking the worst. They will kill you, Johann! Now you have got to fight for your life!

KELLER: Calm yourself. After all, it's a judgment. Not an assassination.

KITTY: It may be an assassination disguised as a judgment.

KELLER: What I have done doesn't deserve that!

KITTY: It's not what you have really done that counts. It's something you carry within you that both frightens and enrages them.

KELLER: You seem to be well informed.

KITTY: Because I am on the outside and I can smell the odor of hatred that surrounds you everywhere. It's your life they want, all of them!

KELLER: I don't believe you!

KITTY: Why not face the situation head on? Now you've got to fight for yourself! A little for me too, if I still exist in your eyes. Won't you ever be able to conceive of happiness apart from these intrigues and acts of madness? Your Kajin . . .

KELLER: Kajin spoke a little too quickly. I would have liked to see him there . . .

KITTY: You would have seen! I reported his exact words to you. He renounces you! His friendship, now you know what it was worth!

KELLER: In a certain way his reaction is quite logical.

KITTY: How can you say that? He's a heartless man. You should accuse him. You ought to put the full responsibility on him. You have very few cards in your favor, Johann. Even your European origin isn't a trump. Just the opposite.

KELLER: Come now, you're becoming frantic.

KITTY: Johann, I am not even trying to distinguish what is good or bad in what you have done. But I alone am with you. All the others want your life! You must defend yourself against them! Be crafty, lie if you have to! Even commit perjury. What does it matter!

KELLER: I would bet it was the lawyer who asked you to say those words to me.

KITTY: How little you believe in me! Do I really need someone to prompt me?

SCENE 7

The same personages plus Hazelhoff who enters abruptly.

KITTY (*Catching herself.*): Ah, it's you? Already . . .

HAZELHOFF: Excuse me . . . My role is a difficult one. I have tried to make it a little less odious.

KITTY: Thank you . . . You have been understanding.

HAZELHOFF (*Gesture toward his watch.*): Impossible to allow you a few extra minutes. Orders, Madam . . .

KITTY (*To Keller purposefully.*): I still have hope, Johann . . .

They shake hands, not daring to kiss in front of Hazelhoff. The latter leads Kitty away and closes the door after her.

SCENE 8

Hazelhoff, Keller.

HAZELHOFF: We have to take up a formality before your departure for Soeliko. A mere formality. We have arrested Sédaria, Kajin's companion. (*He presses a button and rings.*) I am going to have her brought in. It's indispensable that you both be interrogated in one another's presence. (*The door opens behind Keller who doesn't notice it.*) Here now, Keller! Turn around.

SCENE 9

The same characters plus Sédaria, Schultz, policemen, recorder.

HAZELHOFF: You recognize her?

KELLER (*Coolly.*): No.

HAZELHOFF: What? It isn't Sédaria?

KELLER: This is the first time I've seen her.

HAZELHOFF: This isn't the girl who attended your meeting with Kajin?

KELLER: She's not the one.

HAZELHOFF: Not the slightest possibility of error?

KELLER: Not the slightest.

HAZELHOFF: She was captured in a police dragnet. Her papers looked suspicious; the signatures, doubtful. Papers under the name of Selima Amra. But now . . . Our card files are kept current. And it appears that Sédaria and Selima are one and the same. What do you say about that?

KELLER: Your cards must have been mistaken.

HAZELHOFF: All right. But still . . . This girl, finally confused, admitted her name was Sédaria, Kajin's assistant. How does this appear to you?

KELLER: She could have admitted anything you wanted. The police are capable of making a blind man admit he saw the moon!

HAZELHOFF: Bravo! (*He motions to Sédaria who has listened to everything without reacting.*) Step forward then. (*To Sédaria.*) You have already seen this man?

SÉDARIA: Keller.

HAZELHOFF (*To Keller.*): It seems for her part that she knows you. (*To Sédaria.*) You are sure he is the one to whom Kajin had the power station bomb delivered?

SÉDARIA: Since he told you himself . . .

KELLER: That's a lesson learned.

HAZELHOFF: Really! We shall see. (*To Sédaria.*) You are certain you are Sédaria?

SÉDARIA: Yes.

HAZELHOFF: How long have you been actively collaborating with Kajin?

SÉDARIA: Three weeks.

HAZELHOFF: You admit having planted the market bomb?

SÉDARIA: Yes, it was I.

HAZELHOFF: And you met Keller, you spoke with him, you could repeat your conversation?

SÉDARIA: Certainly.

HAZELHOFF (*To Keller.*): What do you say to that? Curious, isn't it?

KELLER: You make that girl say whatever you want.

SÉDARIA: Let's stop clowning, Keller. I confessed who I am. They will never make me say any more than I want to say. But as far as I am concerned, I refuse to protect myself.

HAZELHOFF: Is that a lesson learned, Keller?

SÉDARIA (*Contemptuous.*): Perhaps now he intends to make up for his cowardice!

HAZELHOFF (*Astounded.*): His cowardice?

SÉDARIA: The revolution is a serious thing. Why become involved if your nerves are too weak? Why bother with action if you like to analyze yourself? You think you are freeing the world and you act like a psychologist!

HAZELHOFF: It is true no one forced him! He had a choice.

SÉDARIA: As soon as I saw him I had doubts about him.

KELLER: You hated me from the first moment.

SÉDARIA: I have better intuition than Kajin.

HAZELHOFF: You reproach him, then, for a simple humanitarian gesture?

SÉDARIA: We reproach him for lacking courage!

HAZELHOFF: This lack of courage for killing others, indeed, made him risk his life.

SÉDARIA: Come now! The judges will be dealing with a European this afternoon. Like them. And sensitive. Like them! Not with one of these natives that all the benefits of colonization couldn't improve! "Look," his lawyer will say, "look at the effects of two thousand years of Christianity! A native wouldn't have hesitated!"

HAZELHOFF: You hate him that much!

SÉDARIA: If they spare him, and if I were free, I would do anything to get him, even in the depths of his prison!

HAZELHOFF (*Somewhat amused.*): Ah, young tigress! And all because this man took pity on . . .

SÉDARIA (*Interrupts him with rage.*): We don't need pity! But justice!

SCHULTZ (*Indignant.*): Eighteen dead and twenty-seven wounded by the market bomb alone. That's your justice! Eleven children amputees! All their lives they will never know for what crime or what fault they were punished!

SÉDARIA: The bombs of your air force crushed my village! What crime or fault had my people committed except to refuse humiliation and poverty!

SCHULTZ: Drop this arrogance for a while! If you don't, I'll take you for a walk this afternoon through the hospital wards. And if that sight isn't enough to stir your imagination, I'll leave you alone with the families of your victims. You'll explain to them your concepts of dignity and justice!

A silence.

HAZELHOFF (*To Keller.*): I haven't liked your attempts on behalf of this girl, Keller. What does your attitude mean? Did you really want to save her? But back at liberty she would begin her massacres again! (*Silence.*) I thought you condemned these violent acts, this blind furor!

SÉDARIA: Universal morality, we will respect it when we are free!

SCHULTZ (*To Keller.*): Do you insist on continuing to identify yourself with these individuals?

KELLER: The means they employ is one thing. Their cause is another.

SCHULTZ (*Violent.*): So, you find this cause noble in spite of its excesses! But you condemn the adversary's even in its better aspects! Because it does have some! Will you deny it?

KELLER (*Exasperated.*): You have a man under your boot and you want him to admire the beauty of the leather!

SCHULTZ: In other words, you approve of this despicable person!

KELLER: No! But I know her despair, and if I am separated from her, it's not in order to be on your side! Someone said before I . . .

SÉDARIA (*Interrupting him, sarcastically.*): You'll see, he's going to talk to you about Lenin!

KELLER (*To Sédaria, forcefully and with conviction.*): If multiplying explosions and innocent victims were really enough to bring power to its knees, then what good does it do to educate the masses? What's the good of propaganda? What good are labor organizations, workers' parties?

SCHULTZ (*To the recorder taking notes.*): Write all that down! Word for word!

KELLER (*Still to Sédaria and without worrying about being interrupted by Schultz.*): Why work to create a class consciousness if, to conquer, all you have to do is set off a few sticks of dynamite! That's not counting the fact that you degrade the masses; you give them the feeling that all they have to do is let small groups act, that they don't have to take any initiative, that this action concerns them in a dirty way but does nothing for the future!

SCHULTZ (*To the recorder.*): Write, write . . .

HAZELHOFF (*With a certain irony.*): It's a pity for you, Keller, that these arguments—probably pure Leninist orthodoxy, I don't know— didn't come to mind earlier.

KELLER: I agreed only to an act of sabotage!

HAZELHOFF: You appeared, however, to accept the consequences.

KELLER: I hoped there would be no one in the machine room.

The telephone rings at this moment: three brief, urgent rings. Schultz picks it up.

SCHULTZ: Yes, lieutenant. One minute please! (*He hangs up and to Hazelhoff.*) The escort and car are here, sir.

KELLER: What impatience!

He begins to understand his fate and looks intensely at those around him.

HAZELHOFF (*To Keller.*): Yes, Keller, in a few hours you are going to appear before the justice of your country.

KELLER: The justice of the planters and the big petroleum companies? Justice that's going to·kill this girl, who was pushed to despair and insanity, but that rewarded the flyers whose bombs tore her people apart!

HAZELHOFF (*Irritated.*): Less insolence, Keller! You shouldn't be thinking now of this girl but of yourself.

SCHULTZ: And what sentence do you think you will get?

KELLER: I know, I know! I understand. It took time, but now it's clear. I will appear, it's true, before a tribunal that defends an order I am disturbing! Whichever way I turn (*looks at Sédaria and Schultz who both have the same hostile face)* I find my death desired as if my dying would rid the world of a ghost that frightens it. I could have killed, like all of you. Two miserable coolies more or less among billions of people! And among the millions who die every day on earth without understanding any more about it than they did. I would have been approved by some and hated by others. That is, I would exist, I would be living! But living with a dirty little pain in my heart that so many others find tolerable. And this pain, since I couldn't bear to live with it, now I have to die from it!

He leaves–violently–out the back, followed by policemen, Schultz remaining near Sédaria while the telephone begins to ring again, insistently, during the time of this exit.

(Darkness.)

The lighting that comes on is that with which we are familiar from the nocturnal flashback scenes of each of the four acts. Here we are again in Hazelhoff's home at the end of this day. It is night with moonlight coming through the French door. The judge is encompassed by the light of the lamp. The rest of the stage–deserted– is in the dark. The interruption between Act Four and the epilogue should be as brief as the evacuation of the stage by Sédaria and Schultz and the positioning of Hazelhoff allow.

HAZELHOFF (*Slouched in his armchair, watches Van Rook come into his room through the open French door facing the garden.*): Still as diligent as ever, doctor!

VAN ROOK (*Mops his forehead, opens his bag, chooses his instruments.*): If you don't listen to my advice, soon I won't be able to do anything for you. I move quickly you say? Disease runs even faster!

HAZELHOFF: A hard day, Van Rook! That session at court! Ah, they were in a hurry! Everyone gave the impression he was carrying out a personal vendetta.

VAN ROOK (*Comes near the judge.*): How did Keller bear up?

HAZELHOFF: He spoke very little about himself. You might have said he was trying to forget himself, or was convinced of the futility of words. But at a certain moment, he justified the reasons that caused the rebels to arm themselves.

VAN ROOK: And the lawyer?

HAZELHOFF: Convinced, moving . . . Bah! Keller was sacrificed in advance!

VAN ROOK (*Bitter.*): Sacrificed! And when this . . . "sacrifice" is it . . . actually to take place?

HAZELHOFF: Judgment without appeal. Execution tomorrow at dawn.

VAN ROOK: How did he listen to the sentence?

HAZELHOFF (*Smiling with sadness.*): The way I listened to yours, Van Rook.

VAN ROOK: But you, you believe in God, my dear judge!

HAZELHOFF: And he, Van Rook, he is confident! . . . Confident in a fraternity to be born, just as he is sure that tomorrow morning the sun will rise!

CURTAIN

Keller has just adamantly refused to compromise his principles and inform on his revolutionary comrades or otherwise cooperate with the authorities despite the earnest entreaties of the sobbing Kitty.— Photograph of the Théâtre Royal du Parc production, Brussels, 1966, courtesy of Emmanuel Roblès

Sédaria and Schultz arguing revolutionary justice and the consequences of acts of terrorism.—Photograph of the Théâtre Royal du Parc production, Brussels, 1966, courtesy of Emmanuel Roblès

L'Horloge

(THE CLOCK)

A Dramatic Comedy in Three Acts by

Emmanuel Roblès

Translated by James A. Kilker

TO ARTURO SERRANO PLAJA

Cast of Characters

MATTEOLI *old clockmaker, 65 years old*
VANINA *his niece, 20 years old*
PAOLO *Vanina's boyfriend, 25 years old*
KATIA *procuress, 40 years old*
ELISA *third-floor tenant, 40 years old*
EVA *Elisa's eldest daughter, 17 years old*
MAGDA *daughter of Elisa, 16 years old*
FERRATI *40 years old*
INSPECTOR CARACCIOLO *40 years old*
INSPECTOR FILANGERI *40 years old*

Copyright © 1972 by Editions du Seuil, copyright © 1977 by Southern Illinois University Press.

Caution. Professionals and amateurs are hereby warned that *L'Horloge* (*The Clock*), being fully protected under the copyright law of the United States of America, the British Empire, including the Dominion of Canada, and other countries of the copyright union, is subject to a royalty; and anyone presenting this play without the consent of Southern Illinois University Press will be liable to the penalties by law provided. All applications for the right of amateur or professional production must be made to the Director, Southern Illinois University Press, Post Office Box 3697, Carbondale, Illinois 62901.

This version of the play was performed in Paris, April 10, 1965, by the Compagnie des Deux-Rives, at the Théâtre des Buttes-Chaumont, under the direction of S. Raisonnier.

*In a Mediterranean city at the beginning of the century. The scene
represents the store and workshop of the clockmaker Matteoli. A
door to the left leading to his apartment. A door to the right leading
to the corridor of the building. To the rear a wide window converted
into a showcase through which can be seen the dark, narrow street.
On stands, on shelves, and in showcases: clocks, watches, alarm
clocks. Grandfather clocks, one of which is enormous, near the door
on the right.*

ACT ONE

SCENE 1

*As the curtain rises, old Matteoli is working at his table. It is morn-
ing. Boys can be heard squalling in the street. The old man gets up
and looks out the show-window grumbling:*

MATTEOLI: Dirty brats! Torturing the ragpicker's donkey. The poor
animal . . . They've thrown pepper on her behind again. They'll end
up getting kicked yet. I see Rossetti's boy. And Giuseppe. (*He goes
out. Offstage.*) Will you leave her alone! Little scoundrels! Just wait,
I'm going to flatten you out like rats! Good-for-nothings! (*The noise
moves away. Matteoli comes back to his table muttering.*) Scamps!
Hooligans!

*The sound of chimes. In the renewed silence, from an old clock come
the frail notes of an old-fashioned tune: it is the minuet from "Le
Bourgeois Gentilhomme."*

MATTEOLI: Ah, it's time. (*He gets up, goes to the door leading to the
apartment and calls.*) Vanina! . . . Vanina! Get up! . . . I'm going to
put a glass of milk out for you . . . (*Since there is no answer, he goes
in. Offstage he is heard shouting.*) Vanina, come now! . . . You have
to get up. Vanina. To work . . . (*He comes back on stage a little
haggard.*) She isn't there. God in heaven, where has she gone? How
did she go out? What's happened? Something terrible! Something
terrible has happened. She's always in bed at this hour . . . But the
bed is unmade. Must have left very early. But to go where, great
God? And what does it all mean? . . . (*He walks around in the
room agonizing, without noticing that Vanina has come in through
the corridor door.*) What should I do? But what can I do? . . . I'm

going to notify the police. I'm dead from fright . . . (*He turns around.*) Ah, there you are!

SCENE 2

VANINA: I'm late, Uncle. Excuse me . . .

MATTEOLI: Where were you, I want to know. Nothing happened to you at least? You're very pale.

VANINA: Nothing happened to me. I'm a little tired, that's all.

MATTEOLI: I don't understand. I went to wake you as usual . . . You gave me a terrible scare! That empty room . . . I was . . . Explain it to me.

VANINA: I felt like taking a walk.

MATTEOLI: Are you crazy? . . . Go for a walk at that hour? Everything's still closed. What's this all about?

VANINA: I like the morning: the soft colors of the sky, the fresh smells of another day . . . I walk on the beach, along the piers. I feel strong and something fills my heart. Maybe it's what they call hope.

MATTEOLI: Then, this isn't the first time you've gone out like this?

VANINA: No, Uncle. It isn't the first time.

MATTEOLI: Vanina, Vanina, I ask nothing better than to believe you, you know that . . . But yet . . .

VANINA: You must believe me Uncle Matteoli.

MATTEOLI: A girl, all alone, walking along the seashore before dawn . . .

VANINA: It's simply because I love the sea and I love the dawn . . . Sometimes when the rising sun strikes the waves and sets them aflame, I am certain that a person cannot die without having been happy . . .

MATTEOLI: And you sneak back and get back in bed and I, poor imbecile that I am, I try to awaken you and let myself be touched by so sound a sleep . . . And it's like that every day? . . .

VANINA: Forgive me, Uncle . . .

MATTEOLI: Every day?

VANINA: Almost every day . . .

MATTEOLI: I don't understand . . . I admit this story is past my understanding. My niece goes out her bedroom window every morning on the sly to go for a walk . . . But, you do walk alone at least?

VANINA: All alone . . .

MATTEOLI: Listen, my little girl. I'm just an old fool, but you know how fond I am of you . . . You can speak to me as you would to a father. You're not hiding anything?

VANINA: No, Uncle. I know what you mean. There's nothing else.

MATTEOLI: What foolishness! But don't you know that's dangerous?

VANINA: If I could, I'd spend the whole day away from this rotten neighborhood, away from this house.

MATTEOLI: Vanina . . .

VANINA: Oh, I don't mean to hurt you . . . But these narrow streets make me think of death . . .

MATTEOLI: Let's not exaggerate. It's the smell of fish.

VANINA: You're too old, Uncle, and you no longer hear that call deep within your soul . . .

MATTEOLI: What call?

VANINA: That clamor of the blood that says hurry up, love and live happily so death may come as a friend at the end . . .

MATTEOLI: There's no mistaking . . .

VANINA: Ah, I'd like to get away from here!

MATTEOLI: But where do you want to go?

VANINA (*Suddenly very tired.*): Oh, I don't know! . . . To a country where the air would have that sweetness of dawn that makes your heart tremble . . .

MATTEOLI (*Concerned.*): Vanina, darling, I'm afraid you're going to do something foolish . . .

VANINA: I would like to be very foolish . . . I'd like . . .

MATTEOLI: All right, say it!

VANINA: I would like to go far away . . .

MATTEOLI: Listen! Listen to me closely . . . When your parents died, I became your only family. When I took a wife it was only so she could take care of you; then when I saw she didn't like you, I got rid of her . . .

VANINA: I know.

MATTEOLI: I am living because you're living, Vanina. If you can't be happy . . . here, with me . . .

VANINA: Uncle Matteoli, why don't we go away together?

MATTEOLI: Both of us leave? . . . There, you make me feel good, . . . But you know very well it's impossible.

VANINA: Why? . . . All you'd have to do is sell all this and buy a big trunk with iron rings around it . . . We would go away, we would leave this house. I'd help you. I'd take better care of you than I do now. Oh yes! Uncle Matteoli, we ought to go off together as soon as possible!

MATTEOLI: It's easier said than done!

VANINA: I don't see what the difficulties are. I mean I can't find any that are insurmountable. Oh, Uncle Matteoli . . . we must choose a country on the other side of the world! We have to hurry . . .

MATTEOLI: My little girl, maybe you're not aware of certain things . . . I have commitments to the owner of this building . . .

VANINA: What commitments?

MATTEOLI: I had to sign some papers for Mr. Alfieri . . . I can't sell the shop just like that. All that is very complicated and I'm not going to try to give you a clear explanation. But I am compelled to stay.

VANINA: Is Mr. Alfieri as powerful as they say? Can he really keep you a prisoner here?

MATTEOLI: He is very rich and very powerful and he likes his power.

VANINA: That man whom no one ever sees, whom I've never seen!

MATTEOLI: He lives all the way up there, on the last floor of the building, with his concubines, his bodyguards and that horrible Katia who serves him both as a spy and a procuress. He knows everything that goes on in the building without ever leaving his apartment and there is a certain refinement in the way he exploits his tenants.

VANINA: But that can't go on!

MATTEOLI: It'll go on as long as he does.

VANINA (*Dreamily*.): Am I to understand that it was because of Alfieri that the old organ grinder committed suicide?

MATTEOLI: It was because of Alfieri. He confiscated his organ. The old man hadn't paid his rent in six months.

VANINA: I guessed as much.

MATTEOLI: Most of the tenants, myself included, are closely dependent on him.

VANINA: He must be deformed or sick and find a sort of compensation in being cruel and unjust.

MATTEOLI: No, he's scarcely forty, he's in perfect health, is strong, in fact, and handsome.

VANINA: I have a hard time understanding . . . At any rate, couldn't we escape secretly?

MATTEOLI: But I don't have any money and I owe some large sums to Mr. Alfieri. Without the least effort, he'd have me arrested before I even set foot on a boat.

VANINA (*After a silence.*): If that's the way it is, let's forget these dreams.

MATTEOLI: That's the wisest course, darling. One fine day you will meet a boy you like . . .

VANINA (*Stamping her foot.*): Uncle!

MATTEOLI: I didn't say anything that could offend you. Why are you getting angry?

VANINA: I'm not getting angry. I simply hate your talking to me about those things . . .

MATTEOLI: As you wish. But in the morning when you want to admire the sunrise from the beach, there's no need to go out the window. You can just as well let me know and leave through the door.

VANINA: No, Uncle. I prefer not to let you know and to continue to use the window . . .

Discouraged, Matteoli shrugs his shoulders and goes toward his work bench.

SCENE 3

FERRATI (*Comes in extremely upset.*): Help, my old friend! Help! You've got to help me. You must be with me or I'll lose everything. I'll lose more than life itself!

MATTEOLI: Ferrati, you blockhead! Stop shouting and speak calmly. Explain yourself. What's happened to you?

FERRATI: Ohhh! Matteoli, if you only knew. They're tearing out my soul with a red hot iron. My whole soul. You must help me!

MATTEOLI: I'll do it gladly, but tell me what's going on instead of shouting like a jackass and pulling your hair.

FERRATI (*Plopping down on a stool.*): Old man, there are scoundrels on this earth with souls blacker than Judas'!

MATTEOLI (*Out of patience.*): Get to the point, now to the point! Who has victimized you?

FERRATI: You can't guess? But who, old man, within a radius of seven hundred miles can take pleasure in a dying man's last moments? Who can find delirious joy in another's misfortune? Who can . . .

MATTEOLI: Oh, you're trying my patience! Naturally, it can only be Mr. Alfieri! What kind of trick could he have played on you? Talk quickly and if I can help you I will, but, for the love of God, get hold of yourself and stop this comedy!

FERRATI (*Standing up, indignant.*): Comedy? You know I have a studio on the third floor, third door on the right, for my wood sculpturing . . . with a hand lathe that cost me a fortune and took me three years to pay for. Three years during which my family and I had to eat boiled noodles morning, noon, and night. Three years and nothing but noodles!

MATTEOLI: I understand. Oh, I understand already!

FERRATI: He had everything confiscated!

MATTEOLI: You owed him some money . . .

FERRATI: I signed some promissory notes. He's been preparing his scheme for a long time. Ah, he must be killed! I tell you we should kill him! In a week I could've given his dirty money back to him, but he rushes things. It seems he was spying on me this morning from his balcony while I was shouting with rage and trying to explain to his stooge . . .

MATTEOLI: I'll give you a little drink, something alcoholic.

FERRATI: Leave me alone with your alcohol! I'll kill Alfieri! My family is lost. Everything is lost. I might as well do him in. That will be doing everyone a favor. And you're going to help me. Three years of eating noodles! Three years!

MATTEOLI: Not so fast. I'll do better to take you to a legal adviser. You can tell your story; he will be able to tell you what steps to take.

FERRATI: That's not what I want.

MATTEOLI: It's the only reasonable thing to do.

FERRATI: All the lawyers and advisers in town are on Alfieri's payroll. You know that better than I do.

MATTEOLI: You're exaggerating. The man I know—we'll go to his house right now—(*he takes off his apron*) is completely honest.

FERRATI: Perhaps back when you knew him. He isn't any more.

MATTEOLI: You're coming with me. My niece will watch the shop.

FERRATI: I refuse. I didn't come to see you to go to a counselor. I won't let myself be taken in by a farce like that.

MATTEOLI: What do you expect of me then?

FERRATI: The clock!

MATTEOLI: The clock? What clock?

FERRATI: I want the clock!

MATTEOLI: Are you going crazy?

FERRATI: I know what I'm saying. Do you want me to speak in front of your niece?

MATTEOLI: Hold your tongue! (*To Vanina.*) Don't listen to him.

FERRATI: I was here when the officer came.

MATTEOLI: I can't give you what doesn't belong to me.

FERRATI: He won't be back any more.

MATTEOLI: You don't know anything about it!

FERRATI: He won't come back again and you're taking a risk.

MATTEOLI: We'll see. You're the only one who could turn me in.

FERRATI: Give me that clock! You don't know what I'm going to do with it.

MATTEOLI: I can guess.

FERRATI: It's the best solution. Him and me together.

MATTEOLI: My niece is here, Aldo Ferrati. Be careful.

FERRATI: I'll try once more with Alfieri, one last attempt!

MATTEOLI: I refuse to listen to you.

FERRATI: I'll offer him the clock.

MATTEOLI: Ferrati, be quiet!

FERRATI: It was meant for this kind of mission.

MATTEOLI: Be quiet or go away!

FERRATI: You're running serious risks and that officer won't come back. Give it to me, old man!

MATTEOLI: No. Once and for all, I said no!

FERRATI (*Looking at the clocks.*): If I only recognized it. But the man had his back turned to me. I heard everything from the corridor. I remember everything, but I didn't see the clock.

MATTEOLI: You're nothing but an unfortunate lunatic! Your adventure's affected your mind. You'll have to go see a doctor too, but for the moment let's go get some legal advice.

FERRATI: You don't want to. You don't want to. Please! Give it to me. If the officer never returns what'll it ever be used for?

MATTEOLI: Idiot! Come on now! Vanina, stay here until I get back.

He leads Ferrati away.

FERRATI (*Struggles and comes back in front of the clocks.*): Is it this one, old man? Tell me.

MATTEOLI (*To Vanina.*): Don't pay any attention, his troubles have driven him half crazy. He's delirious.

FERRATI: I am not delirious. If only you didn't have so many things! Maybe it's this one?

MATTEOLI: That's enough!

FERRATI: Or that one with the marble ornament and the golden angels. Tell me, old man, no one would know. I'm telling you that no one would know!

MATTEOLI: Ferrati, come with me or I'll put you out and not do a thing to help a jackass like you.

FERRATI: Well put, old man. Well put. But yours is the solution of a too-cautious man. Too cautious and even a little cowardly. He's got a hold on you too, right? And you're afraid.

MATTEOLI: Don't shout like that! There are already some kids standing in front of the door.

FERRATI: You're afraid. Myself, I don't have anything more to lose. I'm not afraid.

MATTEOLI: Think of your wife and children.

FERRATI: They talk like me. With all their soul they desire the death of Alf . . .

MATTEOLI: Shhh . . . Stupid, you'll stir up the whole neighborhood!

FERRATI: You're afraid.

MATTEOLI: Alfieri has spies everywhere. You're beginning to irritate me. Either you're coming where I want to take you, or you leave and never show yourself here again.

FERRATI (*Pointing to another clock.*): Maybe it's that one with the bronze lion!

MATTEOLI: Let's hurry up. I have work waiting for me.

FERRATI (*To Vanina.*): Don't you agree with me?

VANINA: I don't know what you're talking about.

MATTEOLI: Will you leave her alone! I forbid you to say another word to her.

FERRATI (*To Vanina.*): You don't know Alfieri, eh?

VANINA: I know him by what I hear about him.

FERRATI (*While the old man pulls him by the arm.*): And you don't think he should be killed? Killed, squashed like a poisonous bug!

VANINA: As a matter of fact, I think that would be doing a lot of poor people a favor.

MATTEOLI: You're both crazy! Ferrati, I'm going to throw you out.

FERRATI: Good-bye, Miss! Your answer did me some good. I am happy now! I am . . .

MATTEOLI: Well come on then, imbecile!

FERRATI (*On the threshold to Vanina.*): Good-bye, good-bye! You'll see. If the just want it, the reign of evil will end.

MATTEOLI: But not the reign of lunacy. Get going, you stubborn ass!

They exit.

SCENE 4

While Vanina stares dreamily at the clocks, Paolo comes in cautiously.

PAOLO: Grandfather clocks. Ordinary clocks. Watches. Alarm clocks.

VANINA (*Gives a start.*): Oh, it's you.

PAOLO: Only me. What are you looking at so interestedly?

VANINA: Whatever I feel like looking at.

PAOLO: Bravo! We're going to be able to chat a bit. Finally, you're alone!

VANINA: No.

PAOLO: Sure we can, I saw your uncle go out. He was with that depressing nut Ferrati. Can you tell me where they were going in such a hurry, waving their arms like a couple of idiots?

VANINA: How do you expect me to know?

PAOLO: You don't want to tell me anything? Your mind is made up?

VANINA: Whatever I could tell you, you'd go repeat right away to Mr. Alfieri.

PAOLO: So what? Alfieri is my boss. Everyone has a boss. I'm pretty lucky to have a boss! He pays all right. He's not too demanding and I earn enough to eat all I want.

VANINA: Perhaps it would be better to starve to death than to eat bread earned in certain ways.

PAOLO (*Jeering.*): A lesson on morals now? My dove, the way I earn my bread is my business. Don't worry yourself so much about it. Besides, you don't know what it is to be hungry. Me, between the ages of fourteen and eighteen I went for months eating garbage I found on the wharves. Let's talk about something else . . . and don't give me that look! I know perfectly well you're—how'll I put it?—a little stuck on me. Don't deny it! I read it on your face every time I meet you. I'm used to reading the faces of pretty girls.

VANINA: The day I'm in love with you the statues in the municipal park will start dancing.

PAOLO: Keep on talking. When are you going to get around to opening your damn window for me?

VANINA: You don't get up early enough!

PAOLO: I could come join you in your little bed and teach you a lot of wonderful things you still don't know about or know about only in theory. It's time for you to get around to putting things in practice. I mean, after all, you're not going to stay a virgin all your life?

VANINA: I hope not!

PAOLO: That's what I hope too. Now tell me you'll never belong to anyone else but me. And the sooner the better. I've been watching you Vanina and you know it. You'll be mine or no one's.

VANINA: You haven't been watching me very well!

PAOLO: What do you mean?

VANINA: I'll belong to anyone I want when I want!

PAOLO: When I take you, if you're not a virgin I swear to you I'll strangle you with these hands!

VANINA: You have a unique way of courting a girl.

PAOLO: You probably prefer love songs, serenades with a guitar accompaniment. That's out of style. Me, I say you love me and I enjoy you. So let's make love together.

VANINA: I hate you.

PAOLO: Your eyes say the opposite. You love me. And, Vanina, I think about you lots of times and I have a crazy urge to kiss you.

He takes her in his arms.

VANINA (*Feebly.*): Let me go!

PAOLO: Come now!

VANINA (*Same as before.*): Let me go or I'll call someone.

PAOLO (*Kissing her.*): Your skin is nice and soft and you smell like carnations. (*She kicks him.*) Little slut!

He hops around on one foot, in pain.

VANINA (*Laughing.*): I'll call! I'm going to scream!

PAOLO: My pretty little lamb. You have a delightful body just made for the eyes and pleasures of love. Every night I dream of your breasts, of your thighs!

VANINA (*Wavering.*): Are you going to let me go!

PAOLO: There! But you were beginning to like it. You were trembling in my arms.

VANINA (*Unconvincingly.*): With rage! With disgust!

PAOLO: With pleasure.

VANINA (*Same as before.*): No, no! A thousand times no!

PAOLO: It won't be long before I force your window one of these nights and leap on your bed. You won't even have time to say oof!

VANINA: I'll kill you.

PAOLO: With pleasure!

VANINA: Isn't that old Maria enough for you anymore?

PAOLO: Old Maria! She's only thirty-three. And she makes love like a goddess.

VANINA: Be content with what you have then and leave me in peace.

PAOLO: I don't look like a guy who pays women when he feels like making love. Maria will do until you decide.

VANINA: If I ever dreamed of a considerate, attentive lover, I sure got him!

PAOLO: I tell you, you're too old-fashioned. You read too many French novels.

VANINA: Now get going! And don't ever show yourself to me again!

PAOLO: You could speak to me politely.

VANINA: Get out. My uncle will be coming back. He'll throw you out like a mangy dog.

PAOLO: He doesn't frighten me!

VANINA: Old men don't frighten you!

PAOLO: No one scares me!

VANINA: Even Mr. Alfieri?

PAOLO: What business is that of yours?

VANINA: Mr. Alfieri is powerful. He surrounds himself with strong young men, all at his service.

PAOLO: They're all good pals.

VANINA: Who would only need a signal from their master to break your bones.

PAOLO: That would only happen if I acted against his interests; in that case they would be right.

VANINA: Noble soul! Did you also help put out the old organ grinder? Yes, the one who killed himself?

PAOLO: An old tramp. He earned scads of money begging in front of church doors and he refused to pay his debts. Say! Why don't you want to make love with me?

VANINA (*Unconvincingly.*): Go away! Once more, go away! I hate you!

PAOLO: That's the way girls always talk when the desire between their thighs is bothering them the most. You'll be mine though and no one else's.

VANINA (*Taunting him.*): I'll belong to the man I love!

PAOLO: To me! To me, then! Good-bye. Oh I was about to forget, where did your uncle go?

VANINA: I don't know.

PAOLO: You're lying.

VANINA: That's right. I know exactly where he went with Ferrati. But I won't tell you.

PAOLO: I'll find out.

VANINA: Not from me.

PAOLO: Listen, it's important! Alfieri saw them go out together. He was on the balcony watching Ferrati. I was supposed to follow them. He won't be happy, but I couldn't resist the temptation of having a nice chat with you.

VANINA: Mr. Alfieri will have you beaten.

PAOLO: Idiot!

VANINA: And he might even fire you. You don't deserve the money he's paying you. You're a poor servant.

PAOLO: Come on, come on. Your uncle will soon be back and I'll be able to get it out of him.

VANINA: When you confiscated Ferrati's studio, I mean when you stole it from him, shamelessly plundering him, were you again one of the perpetrators?

PAOLO: No, that time I was busy elsewhere. Mr. Alfieri has more than ninety tenants divided among eleven houses without counting . . . hmm. No need of my talking to you about that. But I'll find out where your uncle went with Ferrati. I'll find out what legal consultant he saw. It'll be easy. I have some irresistible arguments in reserve. Don't you believe me?

VANINA (*Wearily.*): Certainly . . .

PAOLO: Because they could have only gone to a legal adviser. It's child-ish! Fine. I have to leave.

VANINA: Finally!

PAOLO (*He takes her in his arms. She struggles.*): Darling . . . I would have gladly stayed longer. I'm happy near you . . . My beautiful dove. (*He kisses her in spite of her resistance and, ironically:*) I know, I'm making you suffer. Each word from me is a thorn in your heart. But I love you, I can't help it.

He leaves.

VANINA (*Alone, whispers.*): I love you too.

She cries.

SCENE 5

KATIA (*Entering.*): Are you crying Vanina? Why it's true, you're crying. (*Vanina shrugs her shoulders.*) I hope it's not because of that imbe-cile Paolo that I just saw leave here? He's not worth a pretty girl like you ruining her eyes over him. Come now, talk to me. You can tell me everything. I am your close friend.

VANINA: I have nothing to say to you. It's true, Paolo did just leave here, but he hasn't anything to do with my depression.

KATIA: Oh, that's good, that's good! I prefer that. Paolo, as you must know, is a good boy, but he'll never amount to anything.

VANINA: What do you know about it? Besides that doesn't interest me!

KATIA: Of course! Paolo scarcely makes enough to live on. He's lazy. He likes to frequent certain shady side streets where he'll end up catching some nasty disease. He won't have a very pleasant future because one of these days he'll go wrong. You can see it on his face. His sign of misfortune stands out.

VANINA: Why tell me all this? I told you I didn't care about him. There is even one detail that is lacking in your information.

KATIA: Really?

VANINA: He has a mistress. Her name is Maria. An older woman who is past thirty.

KATIA: I know about that. Don't be silly.

VANINA: Stop talking to me about this boy then!

KATIA: All right! All right! I was just saying to myself a girl like Vanina has much better things to do than hankering after that bungler. You are fit for a king, my pretty one. I watch you often. I've seen your bust and hips develop little by little, and today you're just right. It would be a pity for a skinny dog like that Paolo to profit from such a wonderful stroke of luck.

VANINA: That's enough on that. Your words hurt me.

KATIA: You're foolish. Listen, you can tell me everything.

VANINA: Once more, I have nothing to tell you.

KATIA: Not even about your morning escapades out your bedroom window?

VANINA: That doesn't concern you.

KATIA: And your uncle? What if he knew about it?

VANINA: He knows. He knows I go out in the morning to take a walk wherever I feel like. There!

KATIA: You surprise me very much. You walk around like that then, before sunrise through the streets?

VANINA: You're well aware of it Katia, you hypocrite! You've followed me many times as far as the beach or to the jetty. When it was windy, you'd make a face and I could imagine your bad mood. That made me laugh! You must be very angry with a reckless girl like me.

KATIA: Not at all. I also like to walk in the morning to breathe the fresh air off the sea, to look at the beautiful hues of the sky at that time of day. (*She laughs.*) You're not the only one who knows how to appreciate and savor the enchantments of nature.

VANINA: One day it was raining. You hadn't taken your cape. You were soaked and your dress stuck to your legs.

KATIA: I remember.

VANINA: I went out in that bad weather on purpose. I was sure you'd be on my heels. As an additional precaution I brought along a small bag and pretended to look for an address.

KATIA (*With feigned mirth.*): Sly little minx! How mischievous, already at your age. And yet you look so chaste. They'd give you a veil and communion without confession!

VANINA: They could give them to me without confession!

KATIA: Very well. Very well. All right, a word of advice to prove I'm not angry with you: keep yourself away from that Paolo. He is dangerous! He is very inclined toward seducing girls and he's very skillful at the game. You simply must believe you deserve much better than that tramp! Don't let him take you in. Even if you feel your breasts and your belly getting warm. Resist him. Resist him with all your might!

VANINA: You are nice to be so concerned about me and to worry so much about my virtue.

KATIA: I want what's best for you, my child.

VANINA: Thanks again! You're not angry with me because of my walk in the rain?

KATIA: Don't be silly.

VANINA: You might have held a grudge.

KATIA: Of course not. And to prove it to you . . .

She hesitates.

VANINA: And to prove it to me? . . .

KATIA: To prove it to you I'm going to offer you an unhoped-for opportunity. I can introduce you to a man who likes you. A man who wants to make you rich and happy.

VANINA: Ah, there we are!

KATIA: I said rich and happy!

VANINA: He probably wants to marry me?

KATIA: Not exactly. But he has quite a fortune. He's quite in love with you and ready to satisfy your whims. If you are nice to him, obviously.

VANINA: Obviously!

KATIA: He owns apartment houses, bars, an immense apartment and he would cover you with dresses and jewels . . .

VANINA: As far as the dresses and jewelry are concerned, I've already read about that in novels. That's the classical promise to poor girls.

KATIA: But you are poor! Very poor! Your uncle doesn't own anything. Everything here belongs to Mr. Alfieri. If Mr. Alfieri wished, you'd be in the street from one minute to the next with a bundle of clothes over your shoulder and not even enough to eat for three days!

VANINA: But Mr. Alfieri wouldn't do such a thing!

KATIA: No, oh no! He admires you too much.

VANINA: That's certainly what I thought.

KATIA: He often observes you from his balcony. He watches you go off toward the port. In the morning when you appear at the window, he becomes pale and sad . . .

VANINA: I didn't know I was so well looked after. Because he's the one who puts you on my trail to see where I go and what I do.

KATIA: It's quite natural for a man in love.

VANINA: Is he really as rich as you say?

KATIA (*Full of hope and with enthusiasm.*): Even more! This whole district belongs to him. And he's negotiating some very big business transactions.

VANINA: Without even leaving home . . .

KATIA: He's bored anywhere but on the balcony of his apartment. He's somewhat strange. Handsome though, and as intelligent as the devil, but he's bored. However, since he noticed you, he has changed a lot . . . Well? What is your answer?

VANINA: Is he expecting one?

KATIA: Of course, my turtledove. He thinks of nothing else! He was just saying to me a little while ago: are you sure she won't get angry? Will I have a place in her heart?

VANINA: I've made him love me like a schoolboy! A man as powerful as he is!

KATIA: That's it all right.

VANINA: Katia, what an adventure!

KATIA: Say yes right away and you'll never regret it.

VANINA: But I can say no?

KATIA: Ah, these girls nowadays are crazy! If only I'd even come close to a chance like this! Again this morning Mr. Alfieri was worried because he didn't see you come back in. In a very sad way he said to me: Katia, she's late. She must have a lover.

VANINA: Oh, no! This is precisely what he said to you: Katia, there will be a nice reward for you if you bring that little pigeon back to me nice and warm in my bed!

KATIA: Naturally, if you accept he'll have me to thank for it somewhat. I don't see why I should turn down a reward I'd deserve a hundred times over!

VANINA: You're right! You're even hoping that I'll give you a reward too!

KATIA: I know you have a big heart.

VANINA: You're going to lose a lot of money, Katia.

KATIA: Why is that?

VANINA: Because the answer is no!

KATIA: Impossible! You haven't thought it over enough!

VANINA: Poor Katia!

KATIA: You can't give me a flippant answer! It's too important! Too serious!

VANINA: Of course!

KATIA: I am giving you until tomorrow. Think it over carefully! I'll see you tomorrow. You'll go out the window and I'll follow you. We'll talk it all over again as far as the beach. But weigh the pros and the cons! Mr. Alfieri is very powerful.

VANINA: Which means that if I say no, my uncle will also be threatened?

KATIA: You are intelligent! You'll be able to weigh all the risks. As for myself, I'm just an old fool trying to be useful to people. But I am rarely shown any gratitude! See you tomorrow. No, no . . . not another word! See you tomorrow. Besides, I hear someone coming. Good-bye, good-bye!

SCENE 6

Upon leaving Katia bumps into Elisa. Elisa's two daughters, Magda and Eva who are following their mother, are each wearing a white hood and carrying a candle.

ELISA (*Hurling herself at Katia shouting.*): Ah, there you are! There you are! Whore! I'm going to scratch your eyes out! You won't get away!

VANINA: Elisa! For God's sake! What are you doing? Elisa! What's this all about?

ELISA: This viper is the cause of all the trouble. (*To Katia.*) Take this and this and that!

She slaps her, Katia screams.

VANINA: Elisa, please!

ELISA (*Holding Katia by the hair.*): This bitch! She's the one who provides Alfieri with new supplies of flesh! Damn her!

KATIA: Ouch! Let me go! It's not true! Vanina! It's not true! Elisa, let me go, you're pulling my head off!

ELISA: I ought to pull it off for good! Slut! Here's another one!

She slaps her.

VANINA (*Intervening.*): I am asking you to leave her alone, Elisa!

ELISA (*Raging.*): I'm going to squash her like a rat!

VANINA: But what has she done to you?

KATIA (*Crying.*): Don't listen to her! She's crazy!

ELISA: Crazy, me? Repeat that! I dare you to say you didn't lure my daughters to Alfieri's place! They've told me everything. I dare you to say the contrary. But you're going to pay for all that, you female pimp!

KATIA: I haven't done anything! I swear it! You'll go to hell Elisa!

ELISA: You will! The devil will shut you up in a bell that will ring for all eternity! Ah, I could tear off your flesh and expose your nerves and bones! And since you like money so much, I'd like to pour melted gold in your guts! Your soul is more rotten than the body of a dead hyena!

VANINA: Elisa, calm down!

ELISA: No, I'm going to give her a beating! (*But Katia gets away disheveled.*) Ah, it's a good thing! It's a good thing she got away, I would have cut her throat!

SCENE 7

VANINA: Will you explain this to me?

ELISA: I'm going to die from anger. How can a widow avenge herself? That slut succeeded in taking these two innocent girls to Alfieri's!

(*In a rage she removes the hoods from Eva and Magda whose faces appear pale and ashamed.*) Look at them! That horrible female seduced them with her promises of chocolate and gingerbread. They love that and I'm too poor to buy it for them. They went up to Alfieri's place. I was at the washhouse. Mr. Alfieri did what he wanted with them. He, along with his procuress, ought to be burned at a stake drenched in kerosene! And he wasn't alone! He had his friends with him. How could you expect my daughters to resist? My daughters! They undressed them using the pretext that Alfieri wanted to sketch them, that he is a painter of nudes or I don't know what all. And I who watched over them so closely and loved them so! The monsters! One after the other on these poor angels! See their wax faces. They don't have one drop of blood left in their hearts. Alfieri ought to be smothered between two mattresses. I'd take care of the job if somebody would help me. Now what am I to do with these two poor little girls? Who will want to marry them? No one! (*Eva and Magda sniffle and moan.*) We were just on our way to Saint Anthony's church to pray the Lord to erase their shame and purify their bodies. That Katia, I should have torn open her belly with my nails! I am going to pray to God. Perhaps he will perform a miracle. If my two daughters don't become again what they were before, who will take them? You were crying, weren't you?

EVA AND MAGDA (*Slyly.*): Yes, oh yes . . .

ELISA: Isn't it true you pleaded with your executioners to leave you alone?

EVA AND MAGDA (*Same as before.*): Yes, yes . . .

ELISA: And they made you drink?

EVA AND MAGDA: Oh yes!

They elbow one another.

VANINA (*Upset.*): You must go complain to the police!

ELISA: Now that the evil is done? Don't be silly! We have God and only God. We are going to church.

She puts the hoods back on the girls.

VANINA: Go to church! But you also ought to bring charges against Alfieri. My uncle can give you the address of a legal counselor who will help you.

ELISA: Do you think so?

VANINA: Of course!

ELISA: Alfieri and his friends might be condemned to prison?

VANINA: I would think so!

ELISA: Well then, I'll go see this counselor. I would have a little vengeance if those ruffians went to rot alive in a prison cell.

VANINA: Ah! Here's my uncle.

SCENE 8

MATTEOLI (*Seeing the two girls wearing hoods.*): What does this mean?

ELISA: Ah Mr. Matteoli! I wish I were dead!

MATTEOLI: Explain yourself.

ELISA: I was telling your niece how Mr. Alfieri, with the complicity of that nasty shrew Katia, was able to entice my daughters to his place this morning and rape them.

MATTEOLI: Rape them! God in heaven!

ELISA: He had three of his friends with him. And they all did.

MATTEOLI (*Astounded.*): All!

ELISA: Yes, all of them.

MATTEOLI: But that's horrible! The poor children!

ELISA: And I wonder what these creatures will bring into the world? Perhaps monsters, as it so often happens in cases like that. (*Eva and Magda begin crying under their hoods.*) Horned monsters who will make them suffer a thousand deaths. And that's not taking into consideration the fact that I'll have to break my back to feed them. Ah, I would bless heaven if they gave birth to healthy robust boys who could later avenge all three of us!

VANINA: Couldn't they consult that legal adviser? . . . It seems to me that Mr. Alfieri should at least be ordered to make financial reparation. He has millions. This woman is poor and he has aggravated her misfortune in a terrifying way!

MATTEOLI: I can't do anything.

VANINA: Uncle!

MATTEOLI (*Crushed.*): The man I went to see with Ferrati had already been threatened, then bribed. He doesn't want to take on anything against Alfieri.

ELISA: So, my only hope is in God?

MATTEOLI: In God, certainly.

ELISA (*After a sigh.*): Let's go to church right away! If God has seen what happened this morning, I am surprised he hasn't already sent a thunderbolt to pulverize Alfieri and his gang. Let's go to church just the same. And thanks for your kindness, Vanina.

She motions to the girls and leaves behind them.

SCENE 9

MATTEOLI: What a disgrace! What cruelty! What depravation! I think my head is going to explode.

VANINA: Will there never be a man who'll shoot down Alfieri like a mad dog?

MATTEOLI: That monster doesn't even have a soul.

VANINA: If he doesn't have a soul it's not a sin to kill him.

MATTEOLI: Don't say that!

VANINA: I say it because I feel that I'd like to do it myself!

MATTEOLI: Vanina!

VANINA: Oh, I wish I were a boy! I'd run him through the heart with this blade.

She takes one of Matteoli's tools on the workbench.

MATTEOLI: Leave that alone! It's very sharp and it's a tool that costs a lot.

VANINA (*Throwing down the tool.*): If only this house would collapse one day and bury him in the ruins.

MATTEOLI: I'm like you. I would like to see a man as evil as Alfieri get his due, but God will punish him.

VANINA: No, no! Your indignation doesn't last very long. You are already cool-headed again.

MATTEOLI: And you, you're too hotheaded. Like Ferrati. That's crazy. Him too, all he talks about too is killing Alfieri!

VANINA: Maybe he'll do it.

MATTEOLI: I hope not!

VANINA: He was very insistent about a clock. What did he mean? What's that about?

MATTEOLI: Well, about a clock!

He sits down at his workbench and works assiduously.

VANINA: He was strange . . .

MATTEOLI: Let's forget it.

VANINA: Uncle, you are very old and your blood is already slow and cold in your body.

MATTEOLI: Why do you say that?

VANINA: Calm down . . . In the end I'll know why Ferrati wanted that clock so much.

MATTEOLI: I won't tell you.

VANINA (*Dreamily.*): The thing is, we're caught between two choices: leave here or kill Alfieri.

MATTEOLI (*Gives her a look of terror.*): You're hiding something from me!

VANINA: Katia came to talk with me.

MATTEOLI: Katia? When did she come?

Upon these words he gets up. He is all upset.

VANINA: When you were with Ferrati.

MATTEOLI: For God's sake! What did she want? I hope she didn't make you any unsavory propositions! I would get angry!

VANINA: Poor Uncle Matteoli. You're afraid to understand, but you've guessed correctly.

MATTEOLI (*Stunned.*): Lord, what can I do? What can I do?

VANINA: Don't drive yourself crazy like that! Instead tell me why Ferrati wanted so much to have that clock . . .

MATTEOLI: A French naval officer brought it to me two years ago . . . Oh, God . . .

VANINA: Go on . . .

MATTEOLI (*Mops his brow.*): It's a terrible device. It contains a charge of a powerful explosive. I don't know what the officer's purpose was in creating this contraption. He had asked me to devise the timing mechanism so that the explosion would take place on the day and at the hour he would set.

VANINA: And he never came back.

MATTEOLI: Never.

VANINA: And that bomb could really go off at the precise moment you choose?

MATTEOLI: You only have to fuse the device and set the clock accordingly.

VANINA: Oh, Uncle! Look at me! Take courage by looking straight into my eyes!

MATTEOLI: I know what you want.

VANINA: You want the same thing, since you love me, and since you refuse to let me suffer the fate of Elisa's two girls and fall prey to Mr. Alfieri.

MATTEOLI (*Overwhelmed.*): Vanina, I'm dying! The very idea!

VANINA: We'll wait until Sunday morning.

MATTEOLI: Why Sunday morning?

VANINA: Because all the tenants of the building will be at mass.

MATTEOLI: And the others?

VANINA: The explosion will take Alfieri and the bad Christians by surprise. Since God's justice leaves something to be desired . . .

MATTEOLI: You are blaspheming, Vanina! Please!

VANINA: Otherwise, we'll have to do Alfieri's bidding! Is that what you want?

MATTEOLI: No, no! My heart's going to stop!

VANINA (*Ruthlessly.*): Where is that clock?

She walks all around the room.

MATTEOLI: Spare me! Can't we find something else? For instance, you could go take refuge with your cousin in Naples, Alessandro Crispi.

VANINA: Impossible! Alessandro wants to sleep with me too. Last time he came, he forced his way into my room and I had to defend myself.

MATTEOLI: You didn't tell my anything about that.

VANINA: I did a good job of defending myself. My two fingers like a fork in his eyes. Like this! (*She laughs.*) He howled like a dog.

MATTEOLI: I'll beat him if he shows himself in front of me.

VANINA: Let's not think about that anymore. Let's think about our project instead. Can this device really destroy a building like this one?

MATTEOLI: Oh, even a structure twice as big.

VANINA: Good. So that Sunday we'll set the device so that the explosion takes place about an hour after we leave, that means while we're in church!

MATTEOLI: Vanina!

VANINA (*Enthusiastically.*): The four floors will collapse and Mr. Alfieri will disappear!

MATTEOLI: But the innocent, some poor innocent people may be swallowed up in the catastrophe. It's impossible!

VANINA: I will take the precaution of going through all the floors beforehand. Sunday will be the feast of the Virgin. Even the laziest people will be at mass. I'll appear to be motivated by a great fervor and I'll urge the others to go to the ceremony without delay.

MATTEOLI: We will be quickly found out, arrested, and savagely condemned.

VANINA: We won't be found out! What traces will remain? Even the most minute investigation will be useless.

MATTEOLI: What about Ferrati?

VANINA: Ferrati won't talk, you know that.

MATTEOLI (*Shakes his head.*): I can't bring myself to such an extreme solution. You take after your father. All his life he went in for secret societies, assassination attempts, and conspiracies! But me, at my age? It's lunacy!

VANINA: Come on, where is that clock?

MATTEOLI: It's too serious! You don't realize! It's too serious!

VANINA (*Out of patience.*): Uncle Matteoli! (*At this moment chiming is heard. The uncle gives a start, then remains petrified. Vanina smiles. She understands and goes toward the clock. With an expression of delight she listens to a few measures of Lulli's minuet. Then.)* Uncle, that's a charming melody. Very charming. I have always like it . . .

The music continues with the descent of the

CURTAIN

ACT TWO

SCENE 1

As the curtain rises, Matteoli is busy repairing the grandfather clock near the door of the apartment. He looks worried. Vanina comes in. She stops for a moment on the threshold and looks at her uncle attentively.

VANINA: Hello, Uncle.

MATTEOLI: Hello.

VANINA: I'm not too late?

MATTEOLI: I don't think so.

VANINA: I was waiting for a big sailing ship to get under way. It was called the *Annunciation.*

MATTEOLI: I'm not asking you for an explanation.

VANINA: A tug pushed it to the middle of the harbor. Then they set the sails. It began to glide along all white in the sun. From the pier I could hear the sailors singing . . . It made me . . . I felt like shouting! Shouting and singing my fool head off!

MATTEOLI: Your mother liked traveling too. She spent her time making out travel plans while your father drew up black lists or wrote insulting letters to the governor. Anonymous letters, of course. They were both very enthusiastic: she about countries she would never see. He, over revolutions he'd never be able to start.

VANINA: At least they were enthusiastic about something . . . Neither one of them accepted life as they found it. I'm sure they loved each other.

MATTEOLI: Fiercely! How often they fought and stirred up the whole neighborhood. She was deathly jealous and he was as bad as she was. In their home revolutionary posters were on all the walls and photographs of horrible bearded doctrinarians . . . They lived constantly in a setting and atmosphere of melodrama.

VANINA: You're not being very nice to them.

MATTEOLI: I haven't said anything bad. You had to accept them as they were . . . (*He glances at her quickly. She is dreaming.*) Well, what about the sailing ship? . . .

VANINA: It was a four-master bound for Uruguay . . . Uruguay! There must be deep forests, enormous, mysterious rivers . . .

MATTEOLI: You're confusing it with Brazil . . . Uruguay is a country flat as your hand where there is only grass and cattle.

VANINA: Brazil . . . My mother must have liked Brazil too.

MATTEOLI: No. For her the dream land was Arabia. She imagined the forests and rivers to be in Arabia.

VANINA (*By the show window.*): Did you notice the men who seem to be on guard duty on the sidewalk across the street?

MATTEOLI (*Quickly straightening up and coming over by her.*): Men? . . . What men? . . .

VANINA: There . . . You'd think they were watching the house.

MATTEOLI (*Feverish.*): That's the police! There's no doubt they are cops. What does this mean?

VANINA: I don't know. But I think there's cause for concern.

MATTEOLI: You didn't speak to anyone, I hope, about that crazy idea that popped into your head.

VANINA: No one. What are you afraid of?

MATTEOLI: Something strange is going on.

VANINA: I am sure they are there as part of some new scheming trick of Mr. Alfieri!

MATTEOLI: Not so loud!

VANINA: And that idea that today you call crazy hasn't left me. Tomorrow is Sunday. Tonight we will perfect our plan!

MATTEOLI: Again! It seems to me they have let us alone. For pity's sake, don't speak to me anymore about that! Let's make ourselves forget. Let's live quietly. Let's make as little noise as possible. You'll see, they won't think about us anymore.

VANINA: That's your mistake, Uncle. This morning Katia followed me again.

MATTEOLI: What's that you're saying?

VANINA: She came up to me at the end of the pier. It seems Mr. Alfieri is losing patience. He wants an answer without delay.

MATTEOLI: My God, can't they leave poor people in peace? It's already hard enough to live, to make enough to eat every day.

VANINA: Your complaining is quite useless. We have to act quickly. Mr. Alfieri is capable of having me abducted!

MATTEOLI: I refuse to believe it!

VANINA: That's it, stick your head in the sand! But they've concocted something against us. Katia had a funny smile.

MATTEOLI: Then, these men there, outside . . .

VANINA: I don't think they're there because of us, but I don't trust them.

MATTEOLI: That's terrible! What can we do? Lord, what can we do? Ah, I have an idea! I'm going to place you out of harm's way in the convent of the Sisters of the Trinity! There, there'll be no danger. Not that the idea of separating pleases me but it's the only solution.

VANINA: No, they'll take out their vengeance on you, Uncle Matteoli, and in some cruel way. We have to face the situation head on. Here is the only solution.

She designates the little clock.

MATTEOLI: No, no! Not that! What does it matter if they take out their vengeance on me? I am an old good-for-nothing. I don't have much more time to live . . .

VANINA: Don't talk like that. Anyway, you don't think I'm going to spend my best years in a convent and come out at an age when any man worthy of the name won't pay any attention to me!

MATTEOLI: May God give us inspiration and help us!

VANINA (*Ironically*.): He has already given us access to a thunderbolt! And in a machine that counts time. It's obvious.

MATTEOLI: Not so loud . . . They're moving around over there . . .

VANINA: You have to accept the fact that that French officer was sent us directly from heaven!

MATTEOLI: You feel like joking!

VANINA: I am not joking. Watch out!

MATTEOLI: Someone's coming! Someone's running in the hallway!

VANINA: I'm going to see.

MATTEOLI: You're crazy! Stay here . . . I said stay here!

VANINA: It's Ferrati! . . .

MATTEOLI: Ferrati?

Ferrati enters.

SCENE 2

VANINA: Be careful. Men are stationed outside!

FERRATI (*Very disturbed.*): They're there for me!

VANINA: I thought so right away.

FERRATI (*As before.*): Where can I hide? How can I get away from them?

MATTEOLI: What's going on my friend?

FERRATI: I'm being pursued, hunted down . . . The house is already surrounded . . . Hide me quick . . . They're going to come . . . I took a shot at Alfieri!

MATTEOLI: Fool! You killed him!

VANINA: He's dead?

FERRATI: No, my hand was shaking. I missed him! I spent the whole night watching him on the balcony. I was exhausted. He came out of his room. He leaned over toward the street. I fired . . .

MATTEOLI: But where can I put you? I don't see . . . Try my room . . .

VANINA: If they come they'll find you right away.

FERRATI: The tenants on the fourth floor tried to hide me. But they're searching the rooms methodically and they know their business.

VANINA: You're certain you didn't at least wound him? Only a little bit?

FERRATI: No. I tell you I missed him . . . Hide me! I think I hear them . . .

MATTEOLI: I really don't know where to put you.

VANINA: They're not coming yet . . . Why did you only shoot once?

FERRATI: When I saw him, I was . . .

VANINA: He impressed you that much?

FERRATI: He was walking slowly. Wearing a green bathrobe. I never saw him up so close. He has very dark eyes. He seemed to see me even from where I was watching him behind the geraniums . . . Then he leaned over to look down at the street . . . Something went slack inside of me. I raised my arm and I fired. Suddenly he turned around. His face was terrifying. I ran.

VANINA: You should have emptied the revolver on him.

FERRATI: I tell you his face was terrifying!

VANINA (*Kindly*.): You bungled a beautiful opportunity, Mr. Ferrati. And you'll receive the same punishment all the same.

FERRATI (*Frantically*.): No! You are going to hide me. They won't find me. They didn't see me come into your place. They'll believe old Matteoli if he tells them I didn't come in.

VANINA: What did you do with the revolver?

FERRATI: I don't know—I threw it away! I think I threw it in one of those big pots of flowers on the fourth floor landing.

VANINA (*Coldly*.): I'll try to get it back. You never know. There may be a chance to use it again. Too bad your courage abandoned you like that, Mr. Ferrati . . .

MATTEOLI: They're coming. I hear their footsteps on the stairs!

FERRATI: For pity's sake old man . . .

MATTEOLI (*Just a frantic as Ferrati*.): What should I do? God! . . . I have it!

FERRATI: Quick, quick!

MATTEOLI: The clock! This one! Get in and stay still. Hurry up! Above all, don't make any noise! Hold your breath if you have to.

Ferrati gets into the clock. The old man locks the door and throws the key on the table. At that moment inspectors Caracciolo and Filangeri enter. Top hats, moustaches, umbrellas.

SCENE 3

MATTEOLI (*Upset.*): Gentlemen, to what do I owe the honor . . .

CARACCIOLO: Police!

MATTEOLI: What can I do for you?

CARACCIOLO: You can remain quiet and speak only when we ask you questions.

MATTEOLI: I get it! I'll be quiet, I'll be quiet!

CARACCIOLO: An individual ran up this corridor. Perhaps he came in here.

MATTEOLI: Impossible! I'd have seen him. My niece also would have seen him, naturally.

CARACCIOLO: Yeah? Well, he didn't disappear into thin air . . . I'd like to believe you, but you see, I am quite thorough! (*To Filangeri.*) Go take a look around in the apartment . . . (*To Matteoli.*) Excuse us . . . (*He noses around the store.*) That fellow tried to murder Mr. Alfieri but he was only an amateur. He missed him at a distance of fifteen feet!

VANINA: Pity!

CARACCIOLO: What's that?

MATTEOLI: Nothing! . . . She didn't say anything. She was just clearing her throat a little.

CARACCIOLO: Clearing her throat, huh? . . . Well . . . Mr. Alfieri was peacefully taking a breath of fresh air on the balcony. Some pretty girl in the street attracted his attention and he leaned forward and at that very moment: bang! A fanatic jumps up from behind the geraniums and fires. The shot missed his temple by about two fingers.

VANINA (*In spite of signals from her uncle.*): At fifteen feet, what clumsiness!

CARACCIOLO: Mr. Alfieri, never losing his composure, immediately put his people on the murderer's trail. For the moment, though, he's succeeded in eluding them. His mistake was to stay hiding in this building.

VANINA: You said it, he's an amateur. His legs wouldn't carry him any more. He could have run off . . .

CARACCIOLO: Just a minute. Mr. Alfieri recognized him perfectly. We have his description. His complete description. You probably know a man by the name of Ferrati, don't you? He's the one.

MATTEOLI: You don't say? The tenant on the second floor. Who would have suspected? . . .

CARACCIOLO: That's right. It's going to cost him dearly . . . Pretty, that clock!

MATTEOLI (*Wiping his brow.*): Very pretty. Made in France. But this one is more elegant . . .

CARACCIOLO: You think so? . . . I don't find . . .

MATTEOLI (*Ill at ease.*): The other one is Austrian. Marvelous mechanically . . . Do you want to take a look at it?

CARACCIOLO: No, no. I like the French one better.

MATTEOLI: It's just that it's not for sale. It's here to be repaired.

CARACCIOLO (*Amused.*): What does that matter to me? I'm not here to buy a clock from you.

VANINA: Do you know what motives prompted Ferrati to attempt the assassination?

CARACCIOLO: No, not yet. All I'm supposed to do is arrest him.

VANINA: You must know, however, that Mr. Alfieri is, let us say, the opposite of a philanthropist. That he must have pushed Ferrati, like a lot of others, to the point of desperation . . .

CARACCIOLO: Young lady, for the time being my job is limited to trying to capture a man who, in complete disregard for the law, took a shot at another man. The rest is the business of the judges.

VANINA: Mr. Alfieri's misdeeds are too numerous to mention? Strange that justice has so conveniently spared him all this time . . .

CARACCIOLO (*Very curt.*): If that's how you feel, why don't you appear and testify against Mr. Alfieri when the trial of his assassin takes place?

VANINA: I'll do that. Mr. Alfieri has too often occupied himself with disregard for the law . . .

MATTEOLI (*Frightened.*): Don't listen to her Inspector.

CARACCIOLO (*Amused.*): I see, I see . . . If they stage a fireworks display the day they bury Alfieri, I'll know who gave the signal for rejoicing.

VANINA: The fact is, the real victim is the man you're hunting down!

CARACCIOLO: Who cares!

VANINA: You are like God, you're on the side of the rich!

CARACCIOLO: What are you driving at? . . . It's been a long time since the idea of an injustice being committed somewhere has kept me from sleeping.

VANINA: I accept your word for it.

CARACCIOLO: You're a demanding little girl and a bit stupid. To want perfection in this world is to desire the moon. You're going to feel tortured all your life . . .

VANINA: I was just asking myself why you chose this kind of work. In short, you do work in behalf of justice and you don't ever forget it?

CARACCIOLO: I always forget it. I am a policeman strictly by vocation. I put in three years at the police academy and came out with this medal (*he shows it*) bearing the motto Search and You Will Find. In Latin! From my earliest years I loved to play hide-and-seek. I chose a profession that allows me to indulge in my favorite game. A man hides. I am supposed to hunt him out. It's fascinating.

VANINA: Innocent or guilty, it's all the same to you.

CARACCIOLO: You're damn right! I obey orders. It's up to the examining judge to get to the truth. When I was a boy my parents had a big apartment. Looking around this store brings back a memory. My brother and I were playing. One day he hid in the grandfather clock in the dining room. Even before going into the room I had discovered his hiding place. And it was because I no longer heard the ticking of the clock. He had got in the way of the pendulum and this silence had suddenly caught my attention. (*After a short silence.*) Look here, it was a clock like this one . . .

He points to Ferrati's clock.

MATTEOLI: A marvelous piece of furniture, Inspector. It's a work by the famous Buscatelli of Mantua, furnisher to the royal family of Greece and princes of Monaco.

CARACCIOLO: It's imposing! Really, a man could quite easily fit in there!

MATTEOLI: On, no Inspector. It isn't deep enough.

CARACCIOLO: What do you mean, not deep enough? I'm not, of course, considering the possibility of putting a big beer-belly into the thing.

MATTEOLI: Even a slim man, Inspector! Even a very skinny, an excessively skinny man wouldn't fit in there!

CARACCIOLO: Come now! . . . All right, I'll make you a bet. I'm going to call one of the boys waiting in front of the door . . . You'll see! (*He leans over and calls.*) Hey, you there. Yeah, the thinnest one! . . . Yeah! . . . Come over here! (*To Matteoli.*) You're going to see if I'm not right and if he doesn't fit comfortably in that case . . .

Paolo comes in.

MATTEOLI (*Frantic.*): On second thought, I think you're right, Inspector! Completely right!

CARACCIOLO: We are going to proceed with the experiment. (*To Paolo.*) Come this way a little . . .

PAOLO: What am I supposed to do?

MATTEOLI (*To the Inspector.*): Don't go to so much trouble! I believe you! I'm convinced now. One skinny man, I'm sure . . . Even two! Two skinny men!

CARACCIOLO: Let's not exaggerate. Two, no. But one, I'd swear to it.

MATTEOLI: But why bother this good lad? (*To Paolo.*) You'd fit in there, wouldn't you? No need to try.

PAOLO (*Surprised.*): Why do you want me to get in that thing?

MATTEOLI (*Full of hope to the Inspector.*): You see, it's pointless.

CARACCIOLO: No, no you have made a wager. I am meeting the challenge. (*To Paolo.*) Come here . . .

MATTEOLI: Inspector, aren't we going to risk damaging this valuable clock? You know it's very old, very . . . fragile.

CARACCIOLO: Nothing to fear, we will take all possible precautions. (*To Paolo.*) You, scrape your soles carefully . . .

PAOLO (*Obeying but grumbling.*): Okay, but you could have picked someone else . . .

CARACCIOLO (*To Paolo.*): Come on, let's be calm . . . (*To Matteoli.*) Say, where is the key?

MATTEOLI: The key? What do you mean, the key?

At this very moment Filangeri comes in.

SCENE 4

FILANGERI: I found nothing chief.

CARACCIOLO: Too bad! But we sort of thought you wouldn't.

FILANGERI: Just the same, there are some tracks under the window . . .

CARACCIOLO: Tracks? What are you telling me?

FILANGERI: Someone went out the window not very long ago.

CARACCIOLO: Come on, come on, you're dreaming.

FILANGERI: I've already told you, Chief, I never dream even when I sleep. The marks left by the shoes are conspicuous.

CARACCIOLO (*To Paolo.*): Did you see anyone leave?

PAOLO: No one could have gone out that window without our seeing him.

CARACCIOLO: That's clear enough. The question is settled. Well, now, you are going to try to stuff yourself in the case of that clock . . .

PAOLO: What an idea . . .

CARACCIOLO: It's because this gentleman claims a man wouldn't fit in it! Myself, I take the opposite point of view. Try to prove me right.

MATTEOLI (*Frightened.*): But I told you: I'm convinced you have an excellent eye!

CARACCIOLO: No, no! I want to give you proof. Irrefutable proof! Let's see, where is the key? . . . Quick, give me the key!

MATTEOLI (*In a forlorn tone.*): I don't know anymore where I put it . . . I misplace things easily. At my age . . .

CARACCIOLO: Everyone look for the key! You must find it for me at all cost!

MATTEOLI: Someone probably stole it from me. So many people come into this shop . . .

CARACCIOLO: To steal a key like that? . . . Don't give me that!

PAOLO: Say . . . I think it's that one . . .

CARACCIOLO: In fact, it seems to me . . . Give it here . . . Thank you! (*To Matteoli.*) Now, open the clock!

MATTEOLI (*Crushed.*): Perhaps it's not the right key . . . I don't recognize it . . .

CARACCIOLO: Are you going to open . . .

The door opens and Ferrati appears quite startled and in an uncomfortable position.

CARACCIOLO (*Calmly.*): What did I tell you? You can certainly see that a man of normal girth can fit into this clock! I've won my bet.

FILANGERI (*To Matteoli.*): The Chief is a whiz. (*To Caracciolo.*) Chief you're a whiz!

MATTEOLI (*Stuttering.*): Inspector . . .

CARACCIOLO (*To Vanina.*): Do you see, young lady, what you learn at the police academy? (*To Ferrati.*) Come on, Ferrati, you can come out. You're not going to wait in there for the end of the world, are you? (*Ferrati dislodges himself with difficulty.*) Not too stiff? Do a few stretching exercises . . . Like this . . .

He shows him now. Ferrati imitates him mechanically, then, looking sullen, stops.

SCENE 5

CARACCIOLO: My dear Ferrati, your adventure is over. I know people, however, who regret your losing your head at the decisive moment. Isn't that right, Miss?

VANINA: Lady Luck will perhaps smile in the end on other attempts. Mr. Alfieri has made a lot of people hate him and hatred is like running water seeking a slope.

FERRATI: She's right! She's right! Others will try again. Others who are braver and better than I am.

CARACCIOLO: Be careful what you say, both of you. I have to put it down in my report. It can cost you years of prison with nothing but boiled noodles on the menu!

MATTEOLI: Don't listen to my niece. She's a little high-strung. Inspector, I'll have to explain. Her parents were slightly touched in the head to begin with. This unfortunate child inherited their excessive excitability, their inclination for excess, their love for violent attitudes and extreme situations. My brother must have spoken a hundred times a day about killing the enemies of the people. Or more simply, young men who made eyes at his wife. I think, after all, he actually put out the eye of one of her suitors. But mostly his threats weren't to be taken too seriously.

CARACCIOLO: I see she doesn't come from the usual mold. Nonetheless, we'll have to keep an eye on her. There's a sort of fire in her eyes that gives her away. She's aflame, that girl! Burning! Tell me: whose idea was it to hide Ferrati in the clock? I'll bet again, hers.

MATTEOLI (*Piteously.*): It was mine alone, Inspector.

CARACCIOLO: I have to note against you then that you abetted an individual guilty of attempted murder in trying to avoid judicial proceedings.

MATTEOLI (*Alarmed.*): Inspector, allow . . .

CARACCIOLO: Nothing at all. In fact I ought to arrest you, but I'll just ask you to come along to my office.

MATTEOLI (*Whining.*): Is it absolutely necessary?

CARACCIOLO: A simply formality, but indispensable.

MATTEOLI: I have to leave my store then and my niece all alone? . . .

CARACCIOLO: Your niece is capable of her own defense if need be, certainly of taking care of herself several hours without overtaxing her strength. She will watch the store until you return. Let's go . . .

FERRATI: I'm sorry, old man, for having put you in this situation.

VANINA: That's not what you should be most sorry about.

FERRATI: None of this would have happened, old man, if you had listened to me. If you had agreed to turn the little clock over to me.

MATTEOLI (*Glaring at him.*): I don't know what you're talking about.

FERRATI: It's partly your fault. Everything would have been easier.

MATTEOLI: I beg your pardon!

VANINA: You're right but now's not the time to blame one another. Anyway, everything will soon turn out as you wish.

CARACCIOLO: Well said. So let's get going!

MATTEOLI: Take good care of the store. Be patient and wait for me. Don't disturb anything. Don't touch the clocks! The Inspector promised I would be released shortly. We'll be back together this very evening. Isn't that right, Inspector?

CARACCIOLO: It's a promise. Let's go. Good-bye young lady. I think we'll have a chance to see each other again.

VANINA (*Disdainfully*.): I'm not looking forward to it.

CARACCIOLO (*Smirks*.): Keep talking!

VANINA: Is it true my uncle will be back before tonight?

CARACCIOLO: Since it's up to me alone, I promise you that he'll be with you again in an hour or so. Don't worry.

He exits behind Filangeri, Ferrati, and the old man.

SCENE 6

VANINA: He thinks he's being good to me. I'd have preferred just the opposite.

PAOLO: For him to keep your uncle?

VANINA: At least until Monday.

PAOLO (*With suppressed anger*.): Me, if I had my way, he'd be thrown in prison for life. He's got it coming for hiding that scum Ferrati! (*A pause*.) But why mention Monday, may I ask?

VANINA: No, you may not ask . . .

PAOLO: You distrust me, of course . . .

VANINA: I'm not lacking in reasons for distrusting you!

PAOLO: For instance, you wouldn't want to explain to me which clock Ferrati was referring to either?

VANINA: Don't count on it, even if it is unimportant.

PAOLO: My eye, I'll find it in the long run . . . The Inspector pricked up his ears too . . . I'm sure that's all he'll think about. You're not finished with him.

VANINA: If the Inspector's ears pricked up, it's really disturbing. He's more intelligent and discerning than you.

PAOLO: Is this making fun of me going to go on very long?

VANINA (*In a dejected voice*.): I find it amusing . . .

PAOLO: The police have excellent methods for making suspects tell what they want to know.

VANINA: Ferrati won't talk! He's got hold of himself now. No method will loosen his tongue.

PAOLO: But your uncle! . . . After the first slap he'll tell everything! That idiot, when he's a little shaken up, he talks and he talks. He won't stop. You saw how he was awhile ago about your parents? He'll admit everything they ask and even more!

VANINA: My uncle is an old man, but I know he's always brave when he has to be.

PAOLO: So you admit implicitly that this clock story is about something of some importance.

VANINA: A story? I'll tell it to you . . . Once upon a time . . .

PAOLO: You won't be scoffing for long . . .

Frowning, he examines the clocks one by one.

VANINA: Look hard . . .

PAOLO: You both stuck yourselves in a bad mess by hiding Ferrati.

VANINA: Not only in the eyes of the police, of course! Mr. Alfieri must know by now that we tried to protect his murderer. We can expect eviction after, naturally, a seizure in due form of everything in the store!

PAOLO: That's certainly what he ought to do!

VANINA: You will grant me then that I have a right to deplore Ferrati's lack of skill with a revolver.

PAOLO: That guy! If they had left him in our hands he would have spent his days and nights screaming like a man in hell.

VANINA (*Ironically.*): How could he miss a target like that at such a short distance?

PAOLO: Yeah! He was within a half an inch of putting the bullet right in Mr. Alfieri's brain.

VANINA: I'll never be able to console myself for that! And what was your good master doing at that moment?

PAOLO: He was getting a little fresh air. He was looking down at the street.

VANINA: I can give you an even more precise detail: he was waiting for the moment I'd come out the window . . .

PAOLO: You have illusions of grandeur. As if Mr. Alfieri would pay any attention to you!

VANINA: At least to the extent that he sent his faithful Katia to me several times.

PAOLO: Katia? What for?

VANINA: To propose that I join him at his place. I think he's got it in his head to give me lessons in watercolor painting. Unless it's to have me pose in the nude like Elisa's daughters.

Astounded at first, Paolo begins to laugh.

PAOLO: I know your game!

VANINA: Question Katia then!

PAOLO: The boss has never seen you and doesn't even know you exist.

VANINA: Katia will inform you whenever you want.

PAOLO: The boss is interested only in real women, not little girls who know nothing about love and aren't worth a thing in bed.

VANINA: He has changed. It certainly seems he had a wild good time with Elisa's two girls. Yet they knew as little about those things as I do.

PAOLO: I know that story. That was to entertain guests.

VANINA: So that if Mr. Alfieri decided to use me to entertain his guests, you wouldn't object! You would probably take me by the hand yourself and show me what I am supposed to do. If need be, you would help me undress and you would take care of the lighting.

PAOLO: Let's not speak so fast! Mr. Alfieri is a good boss. I'd only have to tell him I want you and he'd never think of you again. If he ever thought of you!

VANINA: Alas! It seems to be all he does all day long and a part of the night.

PAOLO: I know what you're getting at, but I won't fall into your trap.

VANINA: All the same, I am surprised that you react with so much zeal. And to think the other day you threatened me with the worst reprisals if I ever had the intention of belonging to someone else. I will only be yours, you told me. But if it has to do with Mr. Alfieri, then, you have to think things over, right?

PAOLO: Not for Alfieri or anyone . . .

VANINA [*In a certain tone.*]: Tell me at least you'd kill him if he tried to do with me what he did with Elisa's daughters.

PAOLO: You know as well as I that's not even the question. He's not interested in you. He has other worries on his mind at the present time. This Ferrati business is enough to distract him for several days. He must be wondering if it wasn't the work of Amaroucchi the Tunisian and his gang.

VANINA: I know what to expect now! If Mr. Alfieri requests me with particular insistence, as he has done in the case of so many tenants' daughters, I won't dare refuse for fear of seeing my uncle out on the street, his store confiscated! What's more, I can scarcely expect any help from you since it's apparent you approve of the rights of the Feudal Lord!

PAOLO [*Furious.*]: Do you think I'm not wise to you? That you want to turn me against Alfieri?

VANINA: But you are certainly too faithful to him! A man of his calibre! In no circumstance would you turn against him. Even if he took your woman for a night. Well, why not tell him, I'm sure it won't be long before misfortune overtakes him. Where Ferrati stupidly failed, others will succeed.

PAOLO: I'll do that!

VANINA [*Furious.*]: Tell him also that you saw and spoke with me and say I am ready to go up to his apartment whenever he asks for me and to do whatever he wants!

PAOLO [*Threatening.*]: Will you shut up!

VANINA: Question him. Ask if it wasn't me he was spying on this morning from his balcony.

PAOLO: You're crazy. Do you think a person can go up to him and speak to him like that?

VANINA: Well, request an appointment, then. Go through channels!

PAOLO: I have a notion . . .

He raises his hand.

VANINA: Try it! If he is still ready to offer me dresses and jewelry. Ask him!

PAOLO: You're making things up! You're a damn little minx!

VANINA [*Sardonically.*]: Katia's the one who ran the errand. She follows me everywhere, watching me for Mr. Alfieri. Much better than you claim to. Every time she can, she comes up to me to make threats against my uncle mixed with offers from Mr. Alfieri.

PAOLO (*Frantic.*): I don't believe you!

VANINA: Just as I won't believe you when you come here bragging how you'll kill any man competing against you for me.

PAOLO (*Advancing toward her.*): Tonight I want you to leave your window open. Your uncle's room isn't close. He won't hear anything.

VANINA (*Shouting.*): Paolo!

He leaves.

SCENE 7

Vanina closes the clock in which Ferrati had hidden. Chimes of the old clock. Vanina listens to the minuet. Katia comes in.

KATIA: How sad you are, my pretty one!

VANINA: Leave me alone!

KATIA: Because they arrested your uncle Matteoli?

VANINA: They haven't arrested him. He'll be back shortly.

KATIA: Wrong. I just asked. He won't be back so soon.

VANINA: What do you know about it?

KATIA: Eh! He tried to hide Ferrati, that horrible murderer! In the eyes of the law he is an accomplice to an assassination attempt. It might mean prison for years!

VANINA: But the Inspector promised me. He was just going to interrogate him in his office and then release him right away.

KATIA: He won't let him go like that my little dove. That would be too easy. Listen, I just left Mr. Alfieri. He's already informed, you can be sure, and knows your uncle tried to help Ferrati . . .

VANINA: I understand . . .

KATIA: Of course, everything could be very quickly arranged!

VANINA: It won't be arranged the way you're thinking!

KATIA: Your uncle is old. You ought to pity him.

VANINA: I will have pity on him! He wouldn't want freedom acquired at such a price!

KATIA: My you're a stubborn child!

VANINA: You disgust me!

KATIA: I won't say anything more to you.

VANINA: I may no longer have my uncle, but there is someone who can protect me.

KATIA: Who? This Paolo I saw leave here? Is he your boyfriend?

VANINA: He's my boyfriend!

KATIA: Ah . . .

VANINA: And if you keep it up, I'll tell him you're always following me and making me vile propositions!

KATIA (*Pensively.*): All right, all right! It's better if you don't say anything to him. That would complicate everything. Paolo is violent! I didn't realize he was courting you, or that you loved him.

VANINA: He sees me here often.

KATIA: So that's it!

VANINA (*In a cheerful tone.*): If I belonged to someone else, Paolo would kill him and kill me too.

KATIA: What a story! Wait till Mr. Alfieri learns about this!

VANINA (*Same tone.*): Paolo is very jealous.

KATIA: But he must understand that he is Mr. Alfieri's employee, that he owes everything to Mr. Alfieri, the bread he eats and even the air he breathes! I'm going to speak to that one!

VANINA: I never guessed him so dependent on Mr. Alfieri.

KATIA: Mr. Alfieri is very intelligent and he never relies on sentiment. He makes men who work for him devoted not out of fear or because of friendship . . . but because they understand, you see, that without him, Alfieri, they would be nothing. Rejects living in poverty. Yet, just being faithful to their master, they hold a piece of his power right in their grip.

VANINA: And the whole neighborhood hates and fears them. They steal as they pass the merchants' display cases, make passes at the women, beat the husbands, but no one dares say anything to them or complain. But all that will end one day!

KATIA: Mr. Alfieri knows all that will end one day just as life must end, just as the sun must grow cold . . . But he wants to live with the complete freedom of soulless animals.

VANINA (*With sudden violence.*): Tell him to give up trying to have me, that he has everything to fear from me and that I am his most dangerous enemy!

KATIA (*Leaving.*): He'll find that very amusing! What a child you are! If all his enemies—and he has them—were like you, he'd be delighted!

VANINA (*As before.*): Tell him!

KATIA (*On the doorstep.*): I'll tell him, but I know that won't bother him. He'll be waiting for you tonight just the same, just as he does every night!

CURTAIN

ACT THREE

SCENE 1

As the curtain rises, the stage is empty and plunged in darkness. The folding panel of the window showcase is closed. Matteoli and Caracciolo enter.

CARACCIOLO: Hey there! It's dark in here!

MATTEOLI: The panel is closed on the show window. It's Sunday. During the week I open it very early.

CARACCIOLO: You're going to leave it that way. We mustn't be disturbed. I left my assistant on guard by the door.

MATTEOLI: As you wish. At any rate, I don't work on Sundays. In the morning I go to church with my niece and in the afternoon we take a walk along the piers.

He lights a lamp while Caracciolo stands in front of the clock.

CARACCIOLO: Just between us, finding Ferrati wasn't very difficult.

MATTEOLI: You have a good eye . . .

CARACCIOLO: That clock was being repaired and its pendulum was on your table. Why would you have kept it closed eh? I am a graduate of the police academy, my friend.

He shows his medal.

MATTEOLI: I'm sorry for Ferrati. He's a good man.

CARACCIOLO: Good man or not, he's under lock and key. But where's your niece, still in bed?

MATTEOLI: At this time she's probably gone to take her daily walk.

CARACCIOLO: Her walk?

MATTEOLI: Yes. In the morning before the sun comes up she goes out to the beach or to the piers.

CARACCIOLO: She's a funny girl!

MATTEOLI: She was very young when her parents died. I took her in, but I was alone. Then I got married. One day I discovered marks on Vanina's arms and I questioned her. She wouldn't say anything. It was the neighbors who informed me that her stepaunt beat her in my absence. So I had to get rid of the stepaunt and get by as best I could.

CARACCIOLO: But the girl never complained?

MATTEOLI: Never. Already she was too proud for that . . . It won't be long before she's back . . . I have to admit, however, she's been coming back a little late the last few days . . .

CARACCIOLO: Do you know the reason?

MATTEOLI: No.

CARACCIOLO: You haven't tried to find out?

MATTEOLI: Why? I have confidence in my niece! I told you she's an upright and proud girl! But she's suffocating in this house, in this city, and she dreams of a better life far away from here, in a new country. She often goes to see the boats leave for South America.

CARACCIOLO: All that ought to arouse your curiosity.

MATTEOLI: You have to try to understand her. Remember too, she has no one to confide in. I'm old.

CARACCIOLO: What ought to be done, I think, is to get her married as soon as possible.

MATTEOLI (*In a kindly way.*): She'll get married when she wants and to whomever she wants.

CARACCIOLO: I already envy the one who will have the good fortune of domesticating her. She is pretty.

MATTEOLI: What bothers me is that she must be terribly worried over my being kept last night at police headquarters.

CARACCIOLO: It's not my fault!

MATTEOLI: You had promised her I'd be released quickly.

CARACCIOLO: I remember. My intention was simply to interrogate you after Ferrati.

MATTEOLI: Ah! . . . Just the same, you kept me the whole night and I had to sleep on a bench in an evil-smelling room. They put a drunk in around one o'clock in the morning who vomited all over the place. And he kept singing in my face: "My heart is a bird of the islands."

CARACCIOLO (*Bantering.*): That's enough! You're turning my stomach!

MATTEOLI: Without mentioning the rats. Enormous rats! Insolent as could be! I threatened one with my shoe and instead of running he stood his ground.

CARACCIOLO: My regrets.

MATTEOLI: All right. And this morning you come to get me and bring me back home. In a cab! It's enough to confuse anyone! During all that time my poor Vanina must have been as upset as could be.

CARACCIOLO: And if I told you the truth, you'd be even more surprised.

MATTEOLI: Tell me then!

CARACCIOLO: You probably suspected a little that Mr. Alfieri has something to do with it?

MATTEOLI: No, I didn't think about that at all. But what happened?

CARACCIOLO: Well, around noon Mr. Alfieri sent a message asking us to hold you until this morning.

MATTEOLI: Why was that? And can he really give orders to the police?

CARACCIOLO: Listen to me. If he had wanted to have you thrown in prison for a long time, he could. First of all because you hid his assassin! Secondly, because he is on the best terms with the governor, the magistrate, the chief of police, two or three dignitaries of the royal house, and even a prince of the blood!

MATTEOLI: Oh! A royal prince!

CARACCIOLO: You committed an offense. Personally I could close my eyes. But it was easy to have you jailed.

MATTEOLI: Up to that point everything seems rather clear to me. Yet, why did Mr. Alfieri order me held only one night? I don't mean that I am nostalgic for your jail or protesting against my premature release! No. It intrigues me . . .

CARACCIOLO: Perhaps he thought the lesson sufficient.

MATTEOLI: It was! Lord, it was! I won't be able to straighten up for at least three weeks and the memory of the drunk and the rats is going to give me nightmares for a long time . . . Another thing! I could have come home alone . . .

CARACCIOLO: Of course . . . Listen: we interrogated Ferrati a long time. He answered all our questions but we couldn't get anything out of him on one point that personally interests me very much.

MATTEOLI (*Awkwardly.*): He's muleheaded. I know him. It's like that awful idea of wanting to murder Mr. Alfieri! A good man, but really muleheaded!

CARACCIOLO: We let him get some rest last night.

MATTEOLI: That's good! The poor fellow. He must have needed it after that day!

CARACCIOLO: Eh! With him we had to use methods we reserve for those who persist in criminal secrecy! He finally . . . He was very tired. Do you understand?

MATTEOLI: Just what are you telling me?

CARACCIOLO (*Changing his tone.*): I want to know which clock he was alluding to last night. If you don't decide to enlighten me on this subject, I'll wait for your niece who seems to be just as informed as you.

MATTEOLI: You accompanied me back here for that?

CARACCIOLO: Also for that!

MATTEOLI (*After a pause.*): It's a crazy story. One day a French officer paid me a visit—a French naval officer. He brought me this clock for me to work out a device, because his knowledge of clocks was inadequate. The officer never came back for his property . . . Months passed. I had finished the work requested, a rather delicate job, moreover, and my customer never showed up!

CARACCIOLO: Don't go on! I understand. That idiot Ferrati wanted you to make him a present of it. He would have sold it and with the money from the sale he would have been able to pay his debt to Mr. Alfieri!

MATTEOLI: Ah . . . Why yes! That's precisely it!

CARACCIOLO: He wouldn't have been driven to ruin and, in his despair, wouldn't have felt it necessary to fire on his landlord!

MATTEOLI: That's it!

CARACCIOLO: That's it!

MATTEOLI: It's clear!

CARACCIOLO: It's clear! . . . Tell me! Do you take me for a nitwit? I did show you my medal.

MATTEOLI: Inspector!

CARACCIOLO: There's something else behind this. Don't you think I observed your niece yesterday morning?

MATTEOLI: I don't know what you mean.

CARACCIOLO: I want to see that damn clock! And right away! Vanina isn't a girl who looks as if she has a peanut for a brain. I noted that she didn't even protest when I spoke of taking you in. And I could have been easy on you since I had found the man I was looking for. I intentionally made you come with me. And you know, she seemed satisfied.

MATTEOLI: She was satisfied, but I can assure you her face showed the ravages of worry. Vanina feels a strong affection for me, you can be sure about that.

CARACCIOLO: I don't doubt it. That's why I would like to understand. I want to get to the bottom of this clock story.

MATTEOLI: But Inspector, I was beginning to tell you about the French officer . . .

CARACCIOLO: You are a sly one. Trying to take me in with a tale like that. Now where is the clock? Show it to me!

MATTEOLI: I am going to show it to you. But I assure you that two years ago a French naval officer came here with a seventeenth-century clock. One of the first pendulum clocks. In reality, it was a diabolical device . . .

CARACCIOLO (*Gives a start.*): Damn it all! That's it! Where is it? I suspected it was something like that. Hurry up! A diabolical device! I should have thought of it! Idiot that I am! Show it to me right away!

A persistant knocking at the door. Matteoli goes to open. Elisa appears.

SCENE 2

ELISA: I was just going by. I'm glad the police released you, Mr. Matteoli.

MATTEOLI: Thank you. How are your girls?

ELISA (*In a doleful voice.*): Not well. They're with my parents in the country on a little farm lost in the middle of a wilderness of stones. I was coming to get Vanina to go to church.

MATTEOLI: She'll be back before long.

ELISA: Do you know where she is?

MATTEOLI: No . . . You look strange Elisa . . .

ELISA: I do? . . .

MATTEOLI: You can speak freely in front of this gentleman.

ELISA: I haven't anything special to tell you . . . I was just going by. I only wanted to ask Vanina if she would go with me to church.

MATTEOLI: She'll join you as soon as she gets back . . .

ELISA: Yes . . .

CARACCIOLO: Dear lady, if you have something to say to Mr. Matteoli in private, I would be glad to step outside . . .

He goes toward the corridor door.

MATTEOLI (*Worried.*): What is it, Elisa? You are acting strangely.

ELISA (*Quickly and in a restrained voice.*): A saw Vanina last night . . . On the second-story landing . . .

MATTEOLI: Well, what's so extraordinary about that?

ELISA: I call her . . . She was walking as if overcome by fatigue . . .

MATTEOLI: What is this you are telling me? She was worried because I didn't come home.

ELISA: I called her. She came into my place without saying a word. I asked her what was wrong and she gave me a poor forced smile and asked me about my daughters. She was very pale and her hands were shaking . . .

MATTEOLI: What are you getting at? Do you insist on frightening me? I'm sure Vanina will be home at any minute.

ELISA: I hope so with all my heart . . .

She goes toward the door.

MATTEOLI: Elisa!

ELISA: Yes!

MATTEOLI: Where did she go when she left your place?

ELISA (*After staring at him.*): I don't know . . . She probably came back down to go to bed . . . I told you she looked very tired.

MATTEOLI: The emotions of the day exhausted her.

ELISA: That must have been it. Well, good-bye.

MATTEOLI: Elisa . . . Don't leave like that . . . Wait a little. Vanina is going to come home. We'll all go to church together. Wait a little longer . . .

ELISA: All right. I'll be back at my place. You'll let me know. See you in a little while.

She leaves.

SCENE 3

CARACCIOLO: You mustn't worry. Your niece will be back before long. Damn it all, you're used to her morning outings! That woman's mind seems to be a little disturbed?

MATTEOLI: Her two daughters have been victims recently of Alfieri and his friends . . .

CARACCIOLO: Just a minute! What are you telling me?

MATTEOLI: The truth, Inspector!

CARACCIOLO: Good Lord! Check immediately to see if the clock is in its place!

MATTEOLI (*His mind elsewhere.*): What clock?

CARACCIOLO: You know very well! And above all, don't act like an idiot! Where is it?

At this moment Paolo comes in, a Paolo who is haggard and upset.

SCENE 4

PAOLO: Not here?

MATTEOLI: Are you interested in the clock too?

PAOLO: Vanina! Where is she? I looked for her along the beach. No success. I went all around the port. I didn't find her.

MATTEOLI: What do you mean you didn't find her? Why were you looking for her?

PAOLO (*Beside himself.*): Then you don't understand, you old idiot, that she may be in danger!

CARACCIOLO: Don't shout so much young man! A little, calm please!

PAOLO: I recognize you, Inspector.

CARACCIOLO: What's this about?

PAOLO: I came to knock on Vanina's window during the night. She didn't answer. It made me furious, but I figured she was asleep. I knocked loud enough to wake up the deaf. You must have even heard me . . .

MATTEOLI: I didn't sleep here.

PAOLO (*Shouting.*): They kept you all night then?

MATTEOLI: The whole night.

PAOLO: Is Vanina's bed undone? Go see! Hurry up!

MATTEOLI: I should go see if the bed . . . Of course. It's certainly undone! Vanina left as usual before dawn!

PAOLO (*Roars.*): No, she didn't leave before dawn as usual! I stood there waiting all night! She didn't go out!

MATTEOLI (*Bewildered.*): Ah . . . All right, all right . . . I'll go see, I'll go see . . . Who gave you permission to wait for her like that and why . . .

PAOLO (*Furious.*): Go see! Damn it! Go quick!

The old man goes out quickly. Silence. Then Matteoli comes back, alarmed.

PAOLO: Well? Do I have to pry words out of you?

MATTEOLI (*In a broken voice.*): She didn't sleep there last night!

PAOLO: Ah! I thought so! She'll pay for that! I suspected as much. She's stringing me along. She's trying to push me into doing something drastic!

MATTEOLI: What are you talking about anyway and why are you shouting like that?

PAOLO: She must have spent the night with one of her relatives. You do have family in this town? . . .

MATTEOLI: In this town? No, no one. But why do you assume that she went to sleep at a relative's house?

PAOLO: That's enough! I'm going to wait for Vanina right here. As soon as she gets back she'll have to tell me what she has done minute by minute. And I'll check out her activities minute by minute.

MATTEOLI (*Taken aback.*): By what right young man? By what right do you talk like that? Is my niece anything to you? Is she involved with you? It seems to me I should have known. I know Vanina. She wouldn't hide anything from me . . .

PAOLO: Be quiet! Your niece is a hypocrite! She's deceitful! I followed her one day. I saw her go into a church. You know what she did? She went and kissed the statue of the Virgin!

MATTEOLI: So, it seems to me . . .

PAOLO: Let me finish! Do you know where she kissed it? On the belly! That's right, on the belly!

MATTEOLI: Oh! . . .

PAOLO: That's it! Ooooh! Is that all you can say? Eh? And I could cite a hundred things like that. It's like the story about the clock!

CARACCIOLO: What?

PAOLO: The story about the clock. You were there when Ferrati and Vanina talked about it.

CARACCIOLO: Well! Do you know what it's about?

PAOLO: No. But you have to admit it sounds suspicious! That's another one of her ideas. I wonder if it wasn't she who pushed Ferrati into taking a shot at the boss.

MATTEOLI: Wait a minute! Wait a minute! As far as poor old Ferrati's assassination attempt is concerned, I can assure you my niece had nothing to do with it. Ferrati acted on his own, motivated by despair and his hatred for Mr. Alfieri . . .

PAOLO: Yeah! Meanwhile, you'd do well to show that damn clock to the Inspector . . .

CARACCIOLO: Well said, my boy! You've guessed it, it's not just another clock!

At this moment, Katia, in a gay mood, appears in the doorway and comes out with a resounding hello.

SCENE 5

PAOLO: Is that you?

KATIA: Why are all three of you looking so strange?

PAOLO: Come here a minute!

KATIA: What do you want me for? Hurry up! I'm going to church. Today is the feast of the Virgin and I don't want to miss the beautiful ceremony.

PAOLO (*Takes her by the arm and pulls her to the middle of the room.*): Come on! Where's Vanina?

KATIA: How do you expect me to know? Is it my business to act as her chaperon? It seems to me you must be better informed than I am. At any rate, you should be!

PAOLO: Watch how you talk! If you don't tell me where Vanina is I'll squash you like a fly!

KATIA: Help!

CARACCIOLO: Don't worry, dear lady! I'm here!

KATIA: Protect me! Tell him to let loose of my arm! He's hurting me terribly! I'll have bruises the size of dinner plates!

Paolo frees her.

CARACCIOLO: Answer his question just the same!

KATIA: Vanina has reached the age of reason. It seems to me she's free to act as she sees fit. Where is she? Where is she? I don't know a thing about it! She does what she wants to! She doesn't confide in me. I'm not always hanging around her.

PAOLO: You know!

KATIA (*Suddenly very calm.*): If I know, you big idiot, you know too, right?

MATTEOLI: What does she mean? By God, what does she mean?

PAOLO: Perhaps what you don't know old man is that this female pimp works for Mr. Alfieri! And that she has been making sordid propositions to Vanina and pushing your niece into the arms of her boss!

MATTEOLI: Lord!

KATIA: You should talk! He's your boss too! You wanted her for nothing. You tried to have her and every time she slipped through your fingers. So you weren't able to get her for yourself—now go fight over her with the one who was more successful!

PAOLO: You're lying!

MATTEOLI: What are you talking about? My God! What are you talking about! It certainly can't be about my niece?

KATIA: It's precisely about her!

PAOLO: If you have dragged her up there, I'll give you a beating you won't forget!

KATIA: Threats! Always threatening! But you stand there like a simpleton!

MATTEOLI: My God! My God!

KATIA: Go get her then, if you know where she is.

PAOLO: She's going to come home. We'll ask her. You'll see.

KATIA: I feel sorry for you.

PAOLO: She'll pay for it if she's done a thing like that, she'll pay! But I have to hear it from her.

KATIA: Maybe you'll have to be leaving her alone if you know what's good for you. After all, from now on, you'll be up against men. Real men of substance!

PAOLO: I'll take care of you too!

KATIA: I hope I'll be protected in gratitude for services rendered.

PAOLO: So, you admit it!

KATIA: What do you expect me to admit? You and I wear the stamp of what we are right on our faces.

MATTEOLI: I'm not following you very well and all this is not telling me where Vanina is. Now, you seemed to be informed!

PAOLO: You want to know, you want to know where your niece is! Your adorable Vanina! Eh? Do you want to? She's in Mr. Alfieri's bed. Yes, she has spent the night in his bed making love. The whole night! There you are. Now you know. You wanted to be informed, you know. The little whore—for money! Because they promised her dresses and jewelry! Because she would have slept with me if I could have offered them to her! But me, I'm not rich! All I can do is love her! In my own way, but I do love her! I had to be hard and cynical with her because her eyes never blinked, her look sometimes bothers me. And it hurts.

MATTEOLI: Be quiet! It's not true! Be quiet! I don't want to believe she's up there.

PAOLO (*Beside himself.*): For money! Sold herself! Ask Katia. She was the one responsible for making the offers. Dresses and jewelry! Ask Katia if everything I'm saying isn't true. You'll see her again, your little immaculate angel! You'll question your Vanina! She's sure to try to lie, to conceal the truth from you, to tell you about her night in her own way . . .

VANINA (*Who has just appeared in the doorway, tiny and terribly pale.*): No, Paolo, I won't try to hide anything from him . . .

SCENE 6

MATTEOLI: My little girl! My little girl! Whatever you have done, you remain my little girl. Don't tell me anything. I don't want you to talk. All these people are going to leave. We are going to get our things ready. You were right, we should have left this house a long time ago. We will go far away, begin all over.

VANINA: Uncle Matteoli, you are my only friend.

PAOLO: You're going to tell me what you've done. I demand it!

He tries to take her by the arm. She eludes him.

VANINA (*In a low hard voice.*): Don't touch me. I don't want anyone to touch me anymore. I don't want to feel a hand on me ever again.

PAOLO: Well, are you going to talk!

MATTEOLI: By what right do you take that tone with my niece?

PAOLO: By what right! Because she's mine! She belongs to me more than she belongs to you. More than to anyone in the world. Because I love her and because she loves me and only me. (*To Vanina.*) Where did you spend the night?

MATTEOLI (*To Vanina.*): Don't say anything if you don't want to. I'm here. I'll make him go away.

VANINA (*With a sad smile.*): No, uncle. He should know everything. It's true I love him, but if I had belonged to him he would have eroded away my self-esteem. He only needs me to satisfy his own love-starved heart.

PAOLO (*Triumphantly.*): You see, she loves me and she hasn't done anything!

VANINA: Poor Paolo! . . . I really did go up on the balcony last night.

PAOLO (*Darting toward her.*): Vanina!

CARACCIOLO (*Brutally.*): Will you leave her alone!

VANINA (*As in a dream.*): Mr. Alfieri came to open the door. He smiled when he saw me and said he had been waiting. I told him Katia had spoken to me and that I was ready. He answered that he had been waiting for me forever. He was handsome and his voice penetrated my breast like a knife. He was alone and he took me into a big room. He told me he could no longer accept life without me, that it would only be a desert. He took me in his arms and I was his the whole night!

PAOLO: She's lying, she's lying! Now I'm sure of it! Everything she's saying is a lie. Ask Katia! Just ask her! I understand everything. It's because of me she's saying those things. She's testing me. Don't listen to her!

VANINA: If it weren't true, how could I say what I'm going to tell you? He fascinated me as he did in the morning when he watched me from the balcony when I felt his look on the back of my neck, on my shoulders, on my back. I was afraid for him to touch me, as if his flesh against my flesh would completely burn me up. But as soon as he took me against him, something within me began to shine like a pearl, to shine like a diamond.

PAOLO (*Exasperated.*): You see, I'm right! She's forcing herself to find words to make me suffer. I was very hard with her, I never understood her. There's no truth in anything she's saying.

VANINA (*Suddenly growing excited.*): No! Everything is true, everything is true! I swear it! I swear I felt his hands all over my body, on my breasts, on my thighs and he made me burst out of a dark prison where I'd been lying alive and dead at the same time! And this morning, when I woke up against him, he was still sleeping and I placed my head on his chest just at the spot where there was a long scar carved into his flesh as if, during that very night, a flash of lightning had sought his heart!

PAOLO (*Shouting.*): I'll kill him!

He goes out like a crazy man.

CARACCIOLO: Well, he's liable to do something stupid! He's the jealous type! (*In the doorway, he shouts.*) Young man! Come here! Calm down! That's an order! Come back, I say!

He rushes out in pursuit of him.

SCENE 7

KATIA (*Drawing near Vanina.*): Kill Mr. Alfieri, what an imbecile . . . Ah, Vanina, I saw you go up the stairs last night and I was so happy for you . . . I waited. I was afraid you would hesitate and come back down. But I knew you would like Mr. Alfieri. Now here you are a woman thanks to him and, since he loves you, you'll see how he'll make you happy. About Paolo, don't worry . . . The boss can get rid of him quickly . . . You see, my advice was good. Don't look like that . . . Paolo isn't dangerous for Mr. Alfieri. Four floors to climb gives you time to change your mind. And besides, the Inspector will calm him down. See you soon, my little kitten . . .

She exits.

SCENE 8

MATTEOLI: Vanina, we are alone . . . Tell me if you did that for me, so I wouldn't stay in jail . . . so I'd be released.

VANINA: No, don't look for reasons. I don't know what force had been pushing me toward him for days. I knew he was powerful, that he wanted me and that feelings that are insurmountable obstacles for us wouldn't stop him. I still don't know very well why I killed him . . .

MATTEOLI (*Terrified.*): Killed? Vanina! . . . You didn't say that word! I didn't hear correctly.

VANINA: Paolo guessed right. I was lying. I didn't belong to Mr. Alfieri! I killed him.

MATTEOLI: But why, why?

VANINA: Perhaps because alive he negated God's dream! What would life be if love didn't involve us to the very depths of our souls? Last night I followed in Ferrati's footsteps without hiding. Then I looked for the revolver. I hid myself on the balcony behind the geraniums. I saw Mr. Alfieri's men leave and after that I waited. He came out, as he did every morning, at the time I leave for my walk and he leaned over the railing. Then I stood up and he turned toward me and said he had been waiting for me. I fired and he fell. His bathrobe came open over his chest and I saw that scar quite near the heart. The bullet had hit him at one end of the spiral-shaped scar. I bent over him. I saw his frightened look and because I was strong and he was done for, I would have liked to say something consoling to him. (*A pause.*) Perhaps he really loved me, Uncle . . .

MATTEOLI (*Crushed.*): Perhaps, Vanina . . .

VANINA (*After a silence.*): But I did what I had to do, didn't I?

MATTEOLI: Perhaps, Vanina.

VANINA: Neither he nor Paolo knew that love is God's most beautiful gift, did they?

MATTEOLI: I think so, Vanina . . . (*A silence.*) But what are we going to do now? We have to go away, hide.

VANINA (*Dreamily.*): Hide . . .

MATTEOLI (*Tries to lead her away.*): Let's hurry.

VANINA (*Without moving.*): I'm cold.

The noise of hurried footsteps and voices are heard in the corridor.

MATTEOLI (*Tensely.*): They're coming back! . . . In a minute they'll be here to arrest you. They'll take you away!

VANINA: What's going to happen doesn't frighten me anymore.

MATTEOLI (*He goes toward the clock and opens it.*): I know how to activate the fuse on this device! . . . Help me! We have to act fast! Anything is better than falling into their hands!

VANINA (*With a sad smile.*): It's your turn to go to excesses. Will you forget about that clock!

SCENE 9

Caracciolo, Filangeri, Paolo, Katia, Elisa enter running.

CARACCIOLO (*Shouting.*): Leave that clock alone! (*He runs toward the old man and snatches the clock out of his hands.*) Are you crazy?

FILANGERI (*Anguished.*): Be careful, boss!

CARACCIOLO (*Checking the contents of the case.*): All right . . . (*He puts the clock back in its place, then, to Vanina.*) And you, young lady, come along peacefully! Get going! The comedy's over!

VANINA (*Distant.*): That's true. From here on I want to be like those parched-lipped women who remain enclosed behind walls all their lives because they are nothing but love . . .

Vanina goes toward the door. She stops the moment the clock plays Lulli's minuet.

CURTAIN

Vanina and Matteoli in a scene from the first English-language production of *L'Horloge*, which was done from the translation in this volume, performed at South Carolina State College, Orangeburg, in 1972, under the direction of H. D. Flowers.—Photograph courtesy of H. D. Flowers

Left to right: Vanina, Matteoli, and Ferrati. The extremely upset Ferrati is expostulating over Alfieri's seizure of his wood lathe and other tools in payment for promissory notes —notes which Ferrati could have met had he been given a week's extension.—Photograph of the South Carolina State College production, Orangeburg, 1972, courtesy of H. D. Flowers

Left to right: Vanina, Matteoli, Caracciolo, and Filangeri. The two policemen have come to Matteoli's shop seeking the fugitive Ferrati, being sought for the attempted murder of Alfieri.—Photograph of the South Carolina State College production, Orangeburg, 1972, courtesy of H. D. Flowers

Vanina in a pensive moment, as played by Anne Cabon.—Photograph of the Compagnie de Tivoli production, Paris, 1968, courtesy of Emmanuel Roblès

Katia (standing) and Vanina.—Photograph of the Compagnie des
Deux-Rives production, Paris, 1965, courtesy of Emmanuel Roblès

Porfirio

A Farce in Three Acts by

Emmanuel Roblès

Translated by James A. Kilker

TO PAUL GRANDJEAN
AND TO MY COMRADES
OF THE THÉÂTRE DE LA RUE

Cast of Characters

PORFIRIO   30 *years old*
DON PEDRO   50 *years old*
FÉLIX   40 *years old*
GAMELLO   40 *years old*
MANUEL   24 *years old*
MARIFÉ   20 *years old*
JUANITA ˙ 18 *years old*
DOÑA CUMACHA   40 *years old*
THE GENTLEMAN IN GRAY
THE LADY IN PINK
FIRST SOLDIER
SECOND SOLDIER
THIRD SOLDIER
VOICE OF THE PARROT

Copyright © 1972 by Editions du Seuil, copyright © 1977 by Southern Illinois University Press.

Caution. Professionals and amateurs are hereby warned that *Porfirio*, being fully protected under the copyright law of the United States of America, the British Empire, including the Dominion of Canada, and other countries of the copyright union, is subject to a royalty; and anyone presenting this play without the consent of Southern Illinois University Press will be liable to the penalties by law provided. All applications for the right of amateur or professional production must be made to the Director, Southern Illinois University Press, Post Office Box 3697, Carbondale, Illinois 62901.

This farce was performed for the first time March 25, 1953, by the Théâtre de la Rue at the salle Valentin in Algiers, P. Génès directing. In Brussels it was performed May 10, 1960, at the Théâtre de Quat' Sous, with Roland Ravez directing. In Paris it was performed April 8, 1965, under the direction of C. Montechiesi at the Théâtre de l'Alliance Française.

The action takes place in the capital of a Central or South American republic in the heroic era of pronunciamentos. The house of Don Pedro. A large room with whitewashed walls. A massive table. Stools. A window facing the street on the second floor. On the wall a portrait of the president of the Republic, the well-mustachioed General Rosales.

ACT ONE

SCENE 1

DOÑA CUMACHA [*Enters shouting.*]: Juanita! Marifé! No answer. Damn girls! They're not answering on purpose. They want to make me shout myself hoarse. They want to turn my blood sour and make it curdle throughout my body. My throat already feels as if I swallowed a whole nest of hornets! Juanita! Marifé! . . . They couldn't have gone out. Their father has triple-locked the door. But their bedroom is empty. Ah! if they have left the house without being chaperoned, woe unto them! Don Pedro will kill them. Oh! I'm sick! [*She lets herself fall into an armchair.*] When I married their father—may the devil take him!—they were still quite young and I thought I'd be able to train them, make accomplished young ladies of them as the good Lord would want it. But they were already too mean and stubborn for threats and punishment to have any effect. Two heads as hard as an archbishop's staff. [*She gets up.*] Oh! How I'd like to marry them off, get rid of them. But who would want them? And their father doesn't even want to give them a dowry. That malicious, grasping old reptile! [*She calls again with even greater irritation.*] Juanita! Marifé! Where are you, sluts! Vipers!

VOICE OF THE PARROT: Where are you? Sluts! Vipers!

DOÑA CUMACHA: What? . . . Oh, the parrot! Now it's the parrot! That's all I needed. That dirty, mangy-looking, foulmouthed bird! May God forgive me, but he looks just like my first husband! The same profile. It's hallucinating.

VOICE OF BOMBITA: Slut! Viper!

DOÑA CUMACHA: Enough out of you, stupid!

VOICE OF BOMBITA: Enough out of you, stupid!

DOÑA CUMACHA: Oh, my nerves are going to give out. What could I have been thinking of—to marry a widower that age! Sure he's rich, but he'll live another twenty or thirty years. Old men like him seem to be able to keep their balance at the edge of the grave forever! And so stingy he kisses his pesos! He doesn't care for anything but his money and his parrot! He claims that Bombita was born the same day he was! He takes good care of *him*! Even catches flies for him! Married to an old miser, saddled with a filthy parrot and two frivolous, flirtatious, good-for-nothing daughters. That could only happen to me! (*She calls.*) Juanita! Marifé! There's work in the kitchen and my two little doves are hiding God knows where! They ought to have their skirts pulled up and be spanked until their pretty pink bottoms are black as the inside of an old stew pot! . . . Juanita! Marifé!

VOICE OF BOMBITA (*Very excited.*): Juanita! Marifé! Juanita! Marifé! Juanita! Marifé! Juanita! Marifé!

The girls rush in.

SCENE 2

Donã Cumacha, Juanita, Marifé.

JUANITA: Here we are! Here we are!

DOÑA CUMACHA (*Furious.*): So!

MARIFÉ: We're all out of breath!

DOÑA CUMACHA: Where were you, you shameless wenches, you poisonous little spiders? I've been calling you for an hour! One hour! May your father, your grandfather, and all your male ancestors back to the thirty-third generation be damned! . . . Ah! I'm going to faint. I'm dying! (*The two girls hold her up.*) The anguish you cause me! I can already feel my blood turning to vinegar. You'll kill me yet.

She is seated. They fan her.

MARIFÉ: You shouldn't let your emotions get the better of you, Auntie.

DOÑA CUMACHA: You'll kill me, I tell you! And you'll laugh at my funeral. But Saint Polydorus will avenge me. You'll have horns growing on your heads and a beard like that on your chins! And hairs growing out of your noses and ears like eggplants!

JUANITA: Calm yourself, Auntie. You're all red and the veins in your neck are swelling up as big as snakes.

DOÑA CUMACHA: Snakes. That's it. Insult me. You take advantage of the fact that I'm in a coma to insult me! You try to kill me and at the same time . . . Ay! my heart is stopping! I'm going to die! My blood is getting thicker and thicker! How have I offended heaven to be punished like this? A dried-up old husband and two step-daughters as mean as vultures in the laying season!

MARIFÉ: But, Auntie, we came running as soon as we heard your voice.

DOÑA CUMACHA: My voice, you she-devils! It was the voice of the parrot you heard! And he wasn't shouting as loud as I was!

JUANITA: We were in the rear room. It's hard to hear back there. But why get so angry? That could really be harmful to your health.

DOÑA CUMACHA: How I know it! And how happy you would be if it were. You probably pray to the devil every night to make me explode in a fit of anger. Boom! Like one of those smoking toads. Admit it. Admit that you pray to the devil every night!

MARIFÉ: We pray to the Lord to give you better health and a good disposition.

DOÑA CUMACHA: That's enough of your sarcasm! You're both older and worse than your sister! But . . . you haven't told me what you were doing that was so absorbing in that back room? The whole town must have heard me calling you. Everyone but you!

MARIFÉ: We were leaning out the window over the courtyard.

DOÑA CUMACHA: The courtyard window? And what was there so interesting to see, my dear little swallows?

JUANITA (*Animated.*): Don Manuel!

DOÑA CUMACHA: What?

JUANITA: Don Manuel was in the courtyard.

DOÑA CUMACHA: Ah! That's too much! A man in the courtyard and you two girls stand there and admit you were smiling at him from the window. I'm going to tell your father. Don Manuel in the courtyard! And what was that fine looking fellow doing there? Playing a guitar, perhaps?

MARIFÉ: He was giving Doña Isidora's son a botany lesson.

DOÑA CUMACHA (*Shocked.*): A bot, . . . a bot . . . A what kind of lesson?

JUANITA: Botany!

DOÑA CUMACHA: Bot! . . . Oh, Lord! And naturally you were taking it all in! Two decent girls would have gone their way. But you two, of course, stayed. You opened the window as far as you could. And your ears as well. How dreadful! Modesty is dead. What has the world come to? How vulgar!

MARIFÉ: But, Auntie, botany is only the study of plants, of trees and flowers. There's nothing in it that could either shock us or alarm you like this.

JUANITA: It's about the sprouting of seeds, how leaves and buds are created, about stamen, petals, sepals! It's fascinating!

DOÑA CUMACHA: What need do you have to know about either petals or sepals? Does it help you distinguish a cauliflower from an artichoke?

MARIFÉ: Our father is willing to spend all his money on his parrot, but he won't give us a decent education. That's why we're taking advantage of Don Manuel's free lessons.

JUANITA: And he has the wonderful habit of talking in a loud voice.

MARIFÉ: Where's the wrong in that, Auntie?

DOÑA CUMACHA: Where's the wrong? Where's the wrong? I don't know where it is yet, but I'd say it isn't far away . . .

JUANITA: But Don Manuel has been well brought up . . .

DOÑA CUMACHA: That's enough! His father is not on good terms with your father and if he lets you listen to his lessons there must be a catch somewhere. You're just too silly and naïve to know what it is. But I'll keep an eye out! . . .

MARIFÉ: What kind of catch, Auntie? This morning he was merely explaining the structure of the daisy to Doña Isidora's son.

JUANITA: And he dissected one very carefully.

MARIFÉ: I didn't get much out of it, I admit. But Juanita picks up things faster than I do and she learned the whole lesson.

DOÑA CUMACHA: A daisy . . . I see! Luckily you don't know how many indecent things can be said to a girl just by using a daisy!

JUANITA: Really, Auntie?

MARIFÉ: You are very intelligent.

JUANITA: How can you . . .

DOÑA CUMACHA: That's enough girls! Your father's meal isn't ready. Instead of dissecting daisies, go peel some potatoes!

JUANITA: We'll peel them, Auntie.

DOÑA CUMACHA: And light the fire.

MARIFÉ: We will, Auntie.

DOÑA CUMACHA (*Suspicious.*): You are both very strange this morning!

JUANITA (*Ingenuously.*): Not at all. We just want to please you . . .

MARIFÉ: . . . and spare you those fits of temper that are so bad for your liver and your heart!

DOÑA CUMACHA: We'll see. You're being a little *too* good for me . . .

She exits.

SCENE 3

Juanita, Marifé. Marifé goes to check to see whether Doña Cumacha is listening at the door.

MARIFÉ: She's suspicious. Perhaps we did exaggerate a bit . . .

They laugh.

JUANITA: Oh, I'm happy! I feel like jumping, dancing, running! I feel light-headed as a red balloon! I'm like a bale of hay popping in the heat of the sun! Or like a little puddle of clear water that it is evaporating! Oh I feel light! Light! I'm going to disintegrate like a puff of smoke. I'm going to go right up the chimney and into the sky! Watch out! Hold me down!

Marifé takes her in her arms and kisses her affectionately.

MARIFÉ: I am very happy for you, my darling! But we still have to be careful.

JUANITA: Manuel is hiding in the cellar! I left him a whole basket of daisies.

MARIFÉ: Time is going to pass slowly for him.

JUANITA: I'll go be with him a moment.

MARIFÉ: Oh, no! Stay still. If they find him . . .

JUANITA: Tonight we're going to run off together. A car will be waiting for us outside of town. Tomorrow we'll be married. (*She jumps with joy and claps her hands.*) Married! married! married! My father and Doña Cumacha will just have to accept it! What a pity you can't join us tomorrow . . . But you'll be the baby's godmother. Word of honor.

MARIFÉ: Word of honor.

JUANITA: Besides, we're going to hurry.

MARIFÉ: For the baby?

JUANITA: Of course.

Marifé sighs.

JUANITA: Oh! I am so selfish and inconsiderate. Here I am getting you all stirred up.

MARIFÉ: No you're not . . . I mean . . . it's mostly when you tell me how he kisses you on your neck and between your breasts . . . There . . . I mean . . . You shouldn't . . .

JUANITA: Let him do it to me?

MARIFÉ: No. Tell me.

JUANITA: My poor darling . . . You're going to find happiness one day too . . . You'll see! I'm sure of it! I wish it with all my heart! . . .

MARIFÉ (*She sighs.*): Now that we are alone, let's take advantage of it and go over the whole plan. That way we'll avoid any mistakes. So Manuel will remain hidden behind the casks in the cellar until dark.

JUANITA: He has candles and provisions. He'll be able to spend all those long hours pondering over the harmony of the vegetable kingdom in peace and quiet.

MARIFÉ: I'll pretend to go back up to our room.

JUANITA: In reality you will be keeping an eye on our parents while I go rejoin Manuel.

MARIFÉ: You will hold your shoes in your hands so as not to make the steps creak.

JUANITA: And you won't forget to tie my suitcase to a sheet and lower it from the window.

MARIFÉ: But first you will have imitated the cry of a puma on the hunt.

JUANITA: Ah! . . . By the way, what kind of a noise does a hunting puma make?

MARIFÉ: I don't know . . . Perhaps you could meow. That's easier.

JUANITA: All right! . . . I'll meow. The car will be waiting for us at the crossroads.

MARIFÉ: Your disappearance won't be discovered until early tomorrow morning. I'll gain as much time as I can by saying that you must not be feeling very well so you're staying in your room. If all is lost, I'll send father off on a wild-goose chase.

JUANITA: Do you think he'll inform the police?

MARIFÉ: He'll calm down quickly when he learns that Manuel is taking you without a dowry.

JUANITA: But I am only eighteen! Just the same, what would happen if he alerts the police?

MARIFÉ: But, darling, the police will have a lot more to do tomorrow morning than to chase after two people in love who want to get married! They're expecting a new revolution. General Porfirio is supposed to take up arms this afternoon to free the country from oppression. I read the posters.

JUANITA: Oh, my goodness! Won't these disturbances work against our plan? If everything falls apart because of these events, how dreadful!

MARIFÉ: Don't get so panicky! Just the opposite. I'm sure the revolution will help you. Officially, it's supposed to begin at five o'clock. At six, Porfirio will take his oath of loyalty to the constitution. Next the speeches begin. They will go on until dark. Then there will be the banquet, the ball . . . The festivities won't end before dawn. Manuel and you will already be a long way from here.

JUANITA: And what about tomorrow?

MARIFÉ: There will be the parade and more speeches. The whole police force will be called out to protect the cheering sections. You have nothing to fear. Everything will go all right!

JUANITA: In that case: Long live General Porfirio!

MARIFÉ: Not so loud!

JUANITA (*In a confidential tone.*): They say he's very handsome and has a way with women.

MARIFÉ: I only know that he is in command of a magnificent regiment of twenty-nine men. And they all have shoes. All of them!

JUANITA: How exciting! I am going to embroider a handkerchief immediately with the national colors and Porfirio's name. I'll send it to the general to thank him for facilitating my marriage to Manuel.

MARIFÉ: Wait a bit. We're supposed to take care of the cooking . . . Shh . . . Someone's coming (*Don Pedro comes in.*) Ah! Hello, father.

SCENE 4

Marifé, Juanita, Don Pedro.

DON PEDRO (*Furious.*): What's this they're telling me? That you're showing yourselves at the window like a couple of harlots and that you refuse to work? You know I have trouble with my liver and that I am subject to attacks that make my bile back up to my brain! But a lot you care about your father's health. All you think about is causing trouble! Do you want to kill me?

MARIFÉ: I assure you, father, we don't want to kill anyone. It's become an obsession in this house! All we want to do is the right thing.

DON PEDRO: That's why you turn poor Doña Cumacha into a madwoman. Why you smile at young men who come into the courtyard! Why you neglect everything here! You were ordered to go to the kitchen. Are you in the kitchen? No!

JUANITA: We . . .

DON PEDRO: I said no! You talk on and on. You purposely avoid carrying out orders immediately.

JUANITA: When you came in we were just . . .

DON PEDRO: Don't talk back! I forbid you to open your mouth! And another thing, what was that botany lesson all about? Huh?

MARIFÉ: Don Manuel was downstairs . . . in the courtyard . . .

DON PEDRO: Don Manuel in the courtyard and you at the window! Why you're trying to tear my heart out . . .

MARIFÉ: He was giving a botany lesson to Doña Isidora's son and we took advantage of it. Nowadays a lesson costs at least ten pesos!

DON PEDRO: Ten pesos? That's highway robbery! . . . Ten pesos . . .

JUANITA: But it didn't cost you one cent.

DON PEDRO: That's enough! I forbid you to listen to these lessons. Besides, that good-for-nothing Manuel just might come and demand money from me. He'd have the nerve to come and demand ten pesos for a lousy little lesson that you scarcely heard or just listened to absentmindedly . . . I know of cases that are quite similar, but you will pretend not to know about them.

MARIFÉ: Father, please . . .

DON PEDRO: Yes . . . I know what I'm saying. I already owe his father a thousand pesos . . .

JUANITA: You owe a thousand pesos to Don Manuel's father?

DON PEDRO: For eleven years! Eleven years ago a thousand pesos were worth a thousand pesos. Today our currency is worth more. Eleven years ago with a thousand pesos you could buy an automobile. Today you could buy two of them. Do you see how I would lose in the deal?

JUANITA: But you owe him the money!

DON PEDRO: Be quiet. You don't understand anything.

MARIFÉ: Father, you have to give that money back.

DON PEDRO: He doesn't have a receipt. Anyway, I'll wait another eleven years to pay him back if I have to. I'll wait until a thousand pesos are worth a thousand pesos again. If I didn't this would simply be a case of speculation . . . or usury!

MARIFÉ: It's not right, father.

DON PEDRO: What? Two girls who stand at the window over the courtyard and let themselves be taken in are going to talk to me about morality. And do you think I am going to listen to two shameless females who have lost all modesty? I'll have that window boarded over and I'll choose two husbands for you! There's a draft in this house that's blowing caution to the wind. You have to remember that your virginity is your only treasure! I am as poor as a hermit! Now get into the kitchen and be good enough to take care of my little Bombita. Clean his feeding bowl. Be careful not to waste any seed. Ask him if he has eaten well.

MARIFÉ: We will do as you ask. father.

They start to go out.

DON PEDRO: Go on, go on . . . Ah! One more important thing!

MARIFÉ: We're listening.

DON PEDRO: Try to catch a few flies for Bombita. Big yellow ones. The kind that pop. He is very fond of them. On your way, on your way!

They exit.

SCENE 5

Don Pedro.

DON PEDRO [*Alone.*]: What a hell of a life! I can't succeed in marrying my daughters to rich young men. My tenant farmers are robbing me. Taxes are going up. And it's getting harder and harder to conceal my small profits from the tax collectors. What a lot of worries! What anxiety! To top everything off, the revolution is going to break out five hours ahead of schedule. For fifty years our revolutions have begun in the cool of evening when people could go out into the streets after their siesta to acclaim the new president. But a revolution in the midday heat! What an era we are living in! Last week the revolution began at four o'clock and everyone complained. That was insultingly early. What especially worries me are my ten thousand pesos that I didn't have time to convert into dollars this morning. What carelessness! I am really upset. They say this General Porfirio is dangerous! It seems he wants to try out his own personal ideas as far as government is concerned. Up to now all our general-presidents have been good decent imbeciles getting their payoffs from the banana trusts. No surprises with them. They would simply fade away after having filled their pockets. None was ever presumptious enough to experiment with a system he had invented to govern. But Porfirio? Who is paying him to save the country? Let's see. Could it be the Star Company? But it was that company which gave its support to General Rosales last week! Could it be the Deutsch Bananian Company? Or both at the same time? It wouldn't be the first time. General Gonzalez y Tampico managed to be paid by both sides on the sale of the Siguera land. But Porfirio, Porfirio? I'm dying of anxiety! If the rumor that he is poor is true it will be a catastrophe. A poor man who attains power is a thousand times more to be feared than a rich one. Porfirio is capable of blocking bank accounts, or of demanding a special tax to save the nation, or even without going as far as these atrocities, of establishing a voluntary tax to save the country! The anxiety of it all is making my liver swell up and my bile boil! He could also have millions of new pesos printed. And I haven't even converted my ten thousand pesos into dollars. It's enough to make a person cry. I ought to cry—cry as if I had just lost my mother, my poor mother!

Doña Cumacha rushes in.

SCENE 6

Don Pedro, Doña Cumacha.

DOÑA CUMACHA: My heavens, it's happened! We're lost. Dear God, it's begun!

DON PEDRO: What has?

DOÑA CUMACHA: The revolution!

DON PEDRO (*Feverish.*): Calm down, calm down, my dear. The revolution has begun. So, then what?

DOÑA CUMACHA: Don Pedro I'm afraid! I'm scared pink! Or rather, I'm scared red! I mean somewhere between the two. It's making my stomach gurgle.

DON PEDRO: What are you afraid of? What the devil, we've seen plenty of revolutions! They have taken place at the rate of about one every two weeks for a national history that goes back one hundred and twenty years. There are not enough streets, side streets, avenues, public squares, or boulevards to perpetuate the names of all the presidents who have succeeded one another in power since the founding of the Republic.

DOÑA CUMACHA: I'm afraid, Don Pedro. Horrible rumors are going around town.

DON PEDRO: Now you're upsetting me. Are they talking about starting a new tax or a voluntary contribution?

DOÑA CUMACHA: Worse than that!

DON PEDRO: Worse than that? Now I am shaking! Tell me, are they talking about nationalizing the banks? Dear God, please let her say no!

DOÑA CUMACHA: I wish it was just about banks!

DON PEDRO: Out with it! I'm going crazy! Did they say the rich were going to pay? That's only a slogan no one has thought seriously of implementing.

DOÑA CUMACHA (*Striding around the room beside herself.*): I wish it was just about the rich!

DON PEDRO: Come on now, are you going to tell me or not? You can certainly see I'm dying of curiousity. Are they talking about changing bank notes? Tell me quick! At least I hope it's not that. Tell me quick!

DOÑA CUMACHA: Bank notes! Bank notes! Who cares about bank notes!

DON PEDRO: What then? For pity's sake, stop walking around like that! My head will split open like a squash in the fire. Come on, speak! Speak or I'll go crazy right in front of you!

DOÑA CUMACHA: What they're saying . . . Well . . .

DON PEDRO (*Excitedly.*): Yes, yes . . .

DOÑA CUMACHA: They say General Porfirio's troops have received the order to rape all women whose husbands are known to be supporters of Rosales!

DON PEDRO (*Reassured.*): Now, now, my dear. Is that all?

DOÑA CUMACHA: What? You beast! Is that all! You have a portrait of Rosales on the wall. You yelled long live Rosales at this very window at the time of the victory parade! And I would have to submit—at my age! Dear God! This monster says: Is that all! Instead of doing something! Instead of rebelling, of taking up arms! Is that all! Is that all!

DON PEDRO: No my love. I meant it's easy to remedy.

DOÑA CUMACHA (*Beside herself.*): What's easy to remedy? You'd find a battalion of insurgents dishonoring your legitimate wife easy to remedy?

DON PEDRO: First of all, an insurgent battalion is made up of only four men.

DOÑA CUMACHA: Pedro, you are unspeakable!

DON PEDRO: . . . Moreover, I'm going to turn the portrait of Rosales around right away until I can get one of Porfirio. You have to give me enough time, all the same, to get a portrait of the new president! Anyway, I hope that puts your mind at ease.

DOÑA CUMACHA: I see that your mind is more easily put at ease than mine.

DON PEDRO: My dear, you've got to learn to keep a cool head! You've got to face up to reality, what the devil!

DOÑA CUMACHA: Oh yes? Well, Porfirio's revolution is going to be horrible. As horrible as can be!

DON PEDRO (*Crushed.*): But that isn't in keeping with tradition.

DOÑA CUMACHA: It's not like other revolutions. Besides, Rosales doesn't want to give up power. He claims the Star Company still hasn't fully paid him.

DON PEDRO: He's right! This man must be paid. A contract's a contract!

DOÑA CUMACHA: Yes, but Porfirio is at the end of his patience. And he wants to try his system. He's demanding that Rosales leaves the presidential palace at noon. If not, the palace will be shelled!

DON PEDRO: Shelled? Do they have an artillery piece?

DOÑA CUMACHA: A big gun, it seems. The fact that Porfirio has appointed Colonel Gamello commanding general of artillery is proof.

DON PEDRO: Out of nowhere?

DOÑA CUMACHA: Colonel Gamello?

DON PEDRO: No, the gun.

DOÑA CUMACHA: From the museum.

DON PEDRO: Sacrilege! That cannon goes back to the time of Pizarro. A pure historic gem that participated in the conquest of the Empire of the Sun! An evil omen! An evil omen! It might blow up on the first shot. You were right my dear. A horrible revolution is brewing. This Porfirio doesn't respect anything. Pizarro's cannon: A treasure bequeathed to us by our Spanish ancestors. Did you know it's worth more than thirty thousand pesos? That's an official appraisal made by European experts. Thirty thousand pesos are going to be blown up like, that, boom! Blasted to pieces! What an outrage! What desecration. What a crime against history . . . Against the country!

DOÑA CUMACHA (*Bristling.*): Don Pedro, it seems to me you're more disturbed over the fate of that old cannon than you were a moment ago over your wife's honor!

DON PEDRO: No, no my dear! It's not that. But if Porfirio doesn't respect the treasures of the national museum, how can we expect him to respect the personal property and real estate of ordinary citizens?

DOÑA CUMACHA: Just what I was thinking! He won't even respect legally married women. After all, Don Pedro, I imagine you place me in the category of property for which you are most concerned, don't you?

DON PEDRO: Of course, of course. It makes me shiver. What's going to happen? They've pillaged the museum. They'll pillage the banks! They'll loot houses! They'll break open strong-boxes!

DOÑA CUMACHA: Don Pedro, now *you've* got to keep a cool head. You've got to face up to reality, what the devil!

DON PEDRO: Face realities. That's easily said.

DOÑA CUMACHA: That's just how I was going to answer you a while ago.

DON PEDRO: Come now my pet. This is not the time to quarrel. Danger is at our door.

DON PEDRO: Oh! . . . That's true. I hear it already!

Noise outside.

DON PEDRO (*Panicky.*): Already! And the banks are closed!

DOÑA CUMACHA: There they are! I'm leaving. I'm going to hide.

She exits.

SCENE 7

Don Pedro, General Porfirio, General Félix, General Gamello, First Soldier, Second Soldier. General Gamello is carrying a bomb under his arm and never sets it down.

GAMELLO (*Announcing.*): Attention! Attention! Here is General Porfirio! Everyone shout: Long live Porfirio!

DON PEDRO (*Timidly.*): Long live Porfirio!

THE CROWD (*Outside, and very halfheartedly*.): Long live Porfirio. Long live the savior of our country.

PORFIRIO (*At the window and while taking off his gloves*.): Tsk, tsk, tsk, tsk! Not energetic enough! Not enough enthusiasm! I pay you better than Rosales would and you're shirking your assignment. (*He mocks them*.) Long live Porfirio. Long live the savior of our country. Bunch of half-wits! How do you expect to make anyone think this is an outburst of popular enthusiasm? You'd think you were at a funeral mass! First step: you inhale deeply. Fill your lungs. Like this! . . . Second step: you shout "Long Live Porfirio!" (*Pedro jumps*.) There! Not bad considering I'm a little embarrassed at acclaiming myself. But I hope you got the idea.

THE CROWD: Long live Porfirio!

PORFIRIO: That's getting better already.

THE CROWD: Long live the savior of our country!

PORFIRIO: That's fine!

THE CROWD: Long live the liberator of the people!

PORFIRIO: In an hour there'll be a meeting at the public square. Everyone be there! Try to practice a little. No siesta. That makes you soft. And don't get drunk! A want this spontaneous acclamation to be very dignified. Don't forget you're freedom for the people on the march!

THE CROWD: Long live Porfirio!

PORFIRIO: That's good. No more shouting. Enough. You're breaking my eardrums! Get going, get going! (*He turns around*.) Whew! I'm going to set up my headquarters in this house. (*He sees Don Pedro*.) Who is this individual?

FÉLIX: I don't know?

PORFIRIO (*Promptly*.): Have him shot.

DON PEDRO: General, don't do that!

PORFIRIO: Why?

DON PEDRO: You don't shoot a man like that.

PORFIRIO: So! That's what you think? Operetta revolutions are all over with. I want some dead bodies! Like they have in Europe! That makes us look serous!

DON PEDRO: You mustn't shoot me! That's impossible!

PORFIRIO: You're wrong. That's why there are revolutions, so that everything can be possible. I can have you shot if I feel like it! Or appoint you minister, or admiral, or I don't know what all else. Who are you?

DON PEDRO: Don Pedro Panzanaro.

PORFIRIO (*Extending a hand that Don Pedro takes timidly.*): Pleased to meet you! Let's get all the introductions over with at once. Here is General Gamello, the inventor of a magnificent bomb.

GAMELLO (*Swelling up with pride.*): Twelve years of research!

PORFIRIO: At H hour he'll blow up that infamous Rosales and his clique . . .

GAMELLO: Whoof! . . . Up in smoke! . . .

He raises his arm. The bomb falls.

DON PEDRO, THE SOLDIERS: Aye! Aye! aye!

Gamello picks up the device.

PORFIRIO (*Calmly.*): Be careful, my friend. (*After thinking about it.*) Say, shouldn't it have gone off on contact?

GAMELLO: I got hold of it in time.

PORFIRIO: Are you sure?

GAMELLO (*Offended.*): What do you mean, am I sure? Quick, give me a hammer! Twelve years of research! You'll see! No hammer? . . .

He makes as if to throw the bomb. Porfirio restrains him.

PORFIRIO: No untoward displays of wounded vanity. You will await H hour. Is that understood?

GAMELLO (*Very curt.*): I understand.

PORFIRIO: Let's proceed. This is General Félix. General Félix also has invented something. He's the thinker in our revolution. Our theoretician. He has perfected a system of government that will provide happiness for everyone. Nothing but happy people. A republic of happy people! A foolproof system. As soon as I take over, I put it into operation.

FÉLIX: All citizens will sign a form stating that they are happy. Those unfortunates who refuse to sign will be sent to a reeducation camp for a more or less long period of time that will vary according to the gravity of the case. I swear that when they are brought back into society they will be as happy as fish thrown back into the water.

DON PEDRO (*Bewildered.*): Magnificent!

PORFIRIO: Naturally, that isn't the only innovation. A lot of other things will surprise you. You'll see. A golden age is beginning.

At this moment, the voice of Bombita the parrot: "Long live freedom! Long live freedom!"

PORFIRIO (*Startled.*): What's that outrage?

DON PEDRO: It's Bombita.

PORFIRIO: Have him shot!

DON PEDRO: But General . . .

VOICE OF BOMBITA: Long live freedom! Long live freedom! Long live freedom!

PORFIRIO: Have him shot immediately! (*The soldiers rush out.*) He's shouting "Long live freedom!" with too much feeling.

DON PEDRO: Sir . . .

PORFIRIO: He's shouting "Long live freedom!" with too much conviction, too much enthusiasm. It has a ring of defiance to it. Have him shot! . . . That's an order! . . . (*Don Pedro makes a heartbroken gesture.*) I repeat, I'm moving in here along with my general staff while I wait for the infamous Rosales to evacuate the presidential palace and sign a formal resignation. I've just sent him an ultimatum. If within the hour he hasn't signed, I'll order an assault with all my available forces! It'll be spectacular. Gamello, did someone think to notify the photographers?

GAMELLO: It's been done.

PORFIRIO: And the foreign newspaper men?

GAMELLO: That too.

Detonations are heard.

PORFIRIO: There it goes! Blood is beginning to flow. And it's all the fault of that despicable Rosales. (*The soldiers come back in sheepishly.*) Well, boys? Did he die bravely? Did he makes a last request?

FIRST SOLDIER: He asked for a banana.

PORFIRIO: A banana? Well, well. That's out of the ordinary. Generally they ask for a cigarette or a glass of rum.

DON PEDRO: I would like . . .

PORFIRIO: Enough! (*To the soldiers.*) Did he look death straight in the eye?

SECOND SOLDIER: Well, he sort of ruffled up his feathers and . . .

PORFIRIO: His feathers? I don't quite follow you.

SECOND SOLDIER: And then he flew away, General.

PORFIRIO (*Bewildered.*): Flew away?

He moves his arms as if they were wings.

FIRST SOLDIER: Yes sir. We fired on him until our ammunition was exhausted, of course.

PORFIRIO (*Stupefied.*): Of course.

FIRST SOLDIER: But he took shelter on the roof.

PORFIRIO (*Wide-eyed.*): On the roof . . . (*He gets hold of himself and suddenly turns toward Don Pedro.*) Say, do you know this Bombita well?

DON PEDRO: Oh yes sir! . . . I'll have to catch him on the roof!

PORFIRIO: Ah, because you can also . . .

He makes the motions of flying.

DON PEDRO: Oh, no, General!

PORFIRIO: What, then?

DON PEDRO: I'll put his cage on the edge of the roof and, when he gets hungry, he won't be long returning to it. I can attract him also by offering him some yellow flies. He likes them.

PORFIRIO: Ah! Because Bombita, obviously . . .

DON PEDRO: . . . Is my parrot, yes, General.

PORFIRIO (*Glaring.*): What, you wretch! You let us waste all our ammunition on a parrot?

DON PEDRO: I tried my best to tell you. It was you who . . .

PORFIRIO: So that now we have guns but no more ammunition. Not one cartridge! That's a fine piece of work. I can't even have you shot in place of your accomplice. But I have my eye on you. You'll pay for that little trick. I'll have you impaled on the trunk of a coconut palm. I'll feed you to the boa contrictor at the zoo. I'll . . .

At this moment, without a word, Félix hands him the portrait of General Rosales he has just taken down.

PORFIRIO: Treason! Now I understand everything. You're one of Rosales's supporters.

DON PEDRO: There must be some mistake, General.

PORFIRIO: What do you mean, mistake? Isn't that the pig-face of the infamous Rosales? Are you trying to tell me I'm having troubles with my vision? You wouldn't dare say that's a picture of Christopher Columbus. Speak!

DON PEDRO (*Dejected.*): I admit it's a picture of Rosales, but . . .

PORFIRIO: He admits it! There aren't any buts . . . You're married. Where's your wife?

DON PEDRO: Take pity on her, General!

PORFIRIO (*To his two generals.*): Who wants the wife of this traitor?

GAMELLO AND FÉLIX (*Together.*): I do, I do!

PORFIRIO: All right. You can ravish her by alphabetical order, according to size, or by seniority in the highest rank. (*To the soldiers.*) Search the house. She must be hiding somewhere.

DON PEDRO (*Alarmed.*): General, general . . .

PORFIRIO: Not another word out of you! The horns growing out of your head will be thicker than Rosales's moustache.

DON PEDRO: General, I'm not a Rosales supporter. I despise Rosales! I hate him! I spit on him!

PORFIRIO: And this portrait then?

DON PEDRO: That doesn't mean anything. Just one of those unimportant habits you acquire that have nothing to do with your feelings.

PORFIRIO: Really?

DON PEDRO: Putting the current president's portrait up everywhere is just habit. It doesn't mean we're attached to him or to his government. It's just custom.

PORFIRIO: Yes? So that when you hang my portrait here it won't mean anything at all? Just custom? Caramba! You're going to be cuckolded by my whole regiment. You're going to learn to love General Porfirio.

There is a sudden clamor of voices and in his excitement Gamello drops his bomb again. No one sees it. He picks it up, very irritated.

PORFIRIO: Why all the shouting?

FÉLIX: The demonstration you ordered.

THE CROWD: Long live Porfirio! Long live freedom!

PORFIRIO (*Furious.*): It's too soon. It's too soon! I ordered it for an hour later.

VOICE OF BOMBITA: Long live Porfirio! Long live freedom!

FÉLIX (*Leaning out the window.*): That crazy parrot set them off.

PORFIRIO: Send them home. In a little while. Quiet!

But the shouting continues and Porfirio threatens vainly at the window while the curtain falls.

END OF THE FIRST ACT

ACT TWO

SCENE 1

Porfirio, Don Pedro, Gamello, Félix.

PORFIRIO (*Coming back in from the street mopping his brow.*): Finally we got that bunch of zealous loudmouths to shut up. Do you know what kind of an answer they gave me?

GAMELLO: No, Chief.

PORFIRIO: If the revolution isn't over before siesta time, they're all going home. . . . Caramba! What a mentality!

GAMELLO (*Disappointedly shakes his head.*): What a mentality! . . .

His bomb rolls to the floor. He quickly picks it up, but Porfirio, engrossed in his thoughts, see nothing.

PORFIRIO: And furthermore, they told me if I make them work extra hours, they'll make me pay the double-time rate! Can't you just see me doing that? Double time. I'm already having a hard time paying the regular scale. And I'm even beginning to wonder if I can do that up to the end.

GAMELLO: Professional pride is a thing of the past, Chief. I remember, as a boy, following the revolution of a general whose name I forget . . . a big man with a moustache and pistols like—that. *(Making a gesture, he almost drops his bomb. Alarm.)* His insurrection broke out on a Sunday, just before siesta. It so happened, on that day, there was a tremendous bullfight at the arena with Mexican matadors: the Popos brothers. Terrific! A real treat. Well, believe it or not, the corrida was put off an hour so the public could go demonstrate its will to liberate the country and acclaim the new president. This man was decent, mind you, and he took care of everything within a quarter hour. Just before the bullfight he was able to read the names of his ministers. That's the way people were twenty-five years ago! . . .

PORFIRIO *(Bitterly.)*: Yes . . . And today you can't think of starting a revolution on the same day of a most mediocre soccer game, or there'd be no one there to acclaim you. The official photographers would have to cheat and doctor up old photos made at carnival time! . . . Oh, where are those beautiful revolutions of yesteryear? The traditional setting fire to the presidential palace. The looting of banks? When they ravished women the whole night? Today the palace is stone; and the banks have armored doors. And almost all the women refuse to let themselves be ravished. Or they insist on selecting the men who will make them submit to this final outrage. And since they always choose the same handsome ones, one part of the army is dissatisfied and the other is exhausted.

FIRST SOLDIER*(Entering quickly.)*: General!

PORFIRIO: Now what?

FIRST SOLDIER: We've just found Don Pedro's wife!

PORFIRIO: Drag her in here.

FIRST SOLDIER: She's defending herself quite vigorously.

DON PEDRO: Take pity on her, General.

GAMELLO *(To Félix enthusiastically.)*: Let's toss for her, heads or tails!

FÉLIX *(Very excited.)*: Wait, I have a new coin.

But they catch sight of Doña Cumacha and their zeal suddenly vanishes.

SCENE 2

The same, plus Doña Cumacha and the two soldiers.

PORFIRIO: Greetings, Señora! We were just having a friendly conversation with Don Pedro, your husband.

DOÑA CUMACHA (*Furious.*): A friendly conversation? And all the while these beasts were hunting me down in the apartment, calling me an old turtle. And pinching my bottom! I've never been so frightened. I thought they would try to dishonor me.

PORFIRIO: Could that be? Mistreating a nice respectable grandmother like you.

DOÑA CUMACHA (*Ill-tempered.*): I'm not a nice respectable grandmother.

PORFIRIO: Oh, I'm sorry.

DOÑA CUMACHA: And I wonder why these idiots kept telling me your generals would put on a long face when they saw me. Why did they seem to find that idea so funny.

PORFIRIO: My generals? . . . Of course not, of course not. My generals are delighted. Delighted to meet you. Aren't you, gentlemen?

GAMELLO AND FÉLIX (*Forcing themselves to smile.*): Yes, of course. Certainly. Very pleased.

PORFIRIO: You see, most respectable señora.

DOÑA CUMACHA: Once more, I'm not respectable!

DON PEDRO: My dear, you're exaggerating.

DOÑA CUMACHA (*Exasperated.*): I mean I'm not old. My flesh isn't soft and flabby, an overripe banana. My face—thank God—hasn't yet taken on the look of a baboon's behind! And I can still be talked to as a lady able to make a man happy. There!

DON PEDRO: My sweetheart!

PORFIRIO (*Ill-at-ease.*): Of course, of course.

DOÑA CUMACHA (*Unrestrained.*): Those individuals insulted me, scared me half to death. My behind is so black and blue I won't be able to sit down for two weeks.

PORFIRIO: I'd gladly punish them, but I owe them this week's salary. And I can't frighten them too much or they'll go home. I'm going to need their services in a few moments.

DOÑA CUMACHA (*Not listening to him and continuing agitated and furious.*): Pinching an honorable lady's bottom! Chasing the wife of the richest property owner of the region through the rooms of her own house!

DON PEDRO (*Upset.*): My dear!

PORFIRIO (*Interested.*): Really?

DON PEDRO: She's exaggerating. It's her emotions.

DOÑA CUMACHA (*Same as before.*): Yes, my dear husband! This armed rabble all over my petticoats didn't bother you a bit. (*To the generals.*) There's a man who cares more about his money than he does about his wife's honor.

GAMELLO (*Sympathetically.*): How contemptible.

DON PEDRO: But what could I do? Don't you see they're the stronger?

DOÑA CUMACHA: You could've at least protested loudly or put up a fight, I don't know . . . A fight to the death, as if you were protecting your strongbox!

DON PEDRO (*Containing his irritation.*): Come now, Cumacha, you don't know what you're saying. You're spluttering meaningless gibberish. (*To Porfirio.*) She's losing her mind. The shock was too much. Don't listen to her anymore. (*To Cumacha.*) Now, now, it's all over, my love. Go back to your room. Let's be good. Come on now. Back to your room.

DOÑA CUMACHA (*Same as before.*): I'm losing my mind? Oh, I'm losing my mind? You, on the other hand, while they were ravishing me, you remained completely under control! Ah, were I the wife of one of these noblemen, I know he'd have let himself be cut to ribbons on the spot to protect me! To defend my honor! Isn't that right gentlemen?

GAMELLO AND FÉLIX (*Halfheartedly.*): Yes, yes. Naturally. Certainly!

DOÑA CUMACHA (*Triumphantly.*): There! You see? They'd go through the worst kind of suffering, the most horrible torture, rather than let anyone touch the tip of my little finger. They'd have stood up to having their eyes gouged out, their fingernails twisted off, needles pushed through their bellies . . . I don't know what all. Isn't that correct, gentlemen?

GAMELLO AND FÉLIX (*Halfheartedly.*): Yes. Surely. I should say so!

DOÑA CUMACHA: What did I tell you, husband of mine? But you, you only think of your money. Of your pesos, of your endless number of pesos!

DON PEDRO *(Very alarmed.)*: She no longer knows what she's saying. We'll have to send her back to her room. Go get some rest, my little petunia. Right now, my sugar plum.

PORFIRIO *(Interested.)*: No . . . No . . .

DOÑA CUMACHA *(Encouraged.)*: What if I told you he had a bed moved in front of his strongbox where he sleeps every night instead of fulfilling his conjugal duties, according to the Good Lord's commandments! . . .

DON PEDRO *(With a sick smile.)*: Gentlemen, please excuse her. She doesn't know what she's saying anymore! She's raving. She's delirious! It was the shock a while ago. Her brain has all of a sudden gone soft—like wet cardboard. But she'll get over it. I'll call in the best doctor for a consultation. There's not a single word of truth in what she's saying. Don't listen to her! Pure ranting. Plug up your ears. It's unbearable, I know. Excuse her.

DOÑA CUMACHA *(Going toward Don Pedro, threateningly.)*: Not one single word of truth? Not one single word of truth? You dare say there's not one word of truth? Is it true, yes or no, that you've been sleeping next to the strongbox every night for years while I wither away alone in a bed bigger than a parade ground?

DON PEDRO: Her affliction is getting worse! It's taking on frightening proportions! General, we've got to put her to bed. She needs peace and quiet . . . a complete rest. Such absurd stories. I'm poor as Job!

DOÑA CUMACHA: Poor? Him? He's got millions!

DON PEDRO *(Feverish.)*: Go rest, Doña Cumacha. Have some verbena tea prepared for yourself. Quickly, my love, quickly. I'll join you as soon as I've finished talking with these gentlemen.

DOÑA CUMACHA: Millions, do you hear, millions! Bundles of bills like that! I saw them . . . dollars, pounds sterling, pesos . . . through the keyhole. One night, when I was spying, he was clutching them to himself and his face flushed with pleasure. He disgusts me. Worth millions and makes us live like petty municipal clerks!

DON PEDRO: Cumacha, a little self-control!

DOÑA CUMACHA: A little self-control? You had too much a little while ago when these individuals had their hands all over my backside!

Self-control? Do you want me to show you the condition of my bottom? Do you want to see for yourself I'm not lying to you?

PORFIRIO: No need, no need, dear madam! I'll take you at your word . . . and please believe me when I tell you how sorry I am. It was an unfortunate misunderstanding. Please be good enough to go for a little rest.

DON PEDRO (*Briskly.*): That's it. The very thing. A little rest!

Doña Cumacha exits.

PORFIRIO (*To the generals and soldiers.*): All of you, from here on try to conduct yourselves as real noblemen. Continue searching the house, but with a little tact, a little refinement. Some regal *savoir-faire*, what the devil! On your way, on your way . . . .

SCENE 3

Porfirio, Don Pedro.

DON PEDRO: Excellency, I hope you didn't believe a word that unfortunate woman said. She had a fever. It was fear, you understand? Tell me at least you didn't believe her.

PORFIRIO: I've got a lot of other worries and her remarks, dear sir, have almost completely gone out of my mind. Your poor wife . . .

DON PEDRO (*Briskly.*): You don't have to "sir" me, Excellency. I like the familiarity of the soldier.

PORFIRIO: No, no, Don Pedro. You have a right to the respect due your age . . . your position.

DON PEDRO (*Alarmed.*): Not at all, please. I'm a poor man. I'd be very happy if you'd treat me like an ordinary citizen! You speak as if I were an important person. I'm just a lowly worm.

PORFIRIO (*Preoccupied.*): Let's change the subject, Don Pedro.

DON PEDRO: But before my wife came you were kind enough to talk as casually to me as you do to everyone else. Do you feel less friendly toward me now? less esteem?

PORFIRIO: Just the opposite, Don Pedro, just the opposite! I have a lot of respect for you and I'll prove it. But time is passing and Rosales still hasn't answered my ultimatum. If in exactly thirty-five minutes he still hasn't resigned, I'll have to launch an assault on the presidential palace. This is the solution I personally like, but I'm not so sure my troops go for it. Anyway . . . I'm not leading this revolution for the sake of personal ambition, though power and glory do have a certain appeal. I want happiness for the greatest number. I want to fully implement the theories of my friend, Félix. With a little common sense, method, good organization, and a few camps for the more reluctant in spirit, I am convinced we'll succeed in making all our fellow citizens happy.

DON PEDRO: A generous man and a noble soul! I wish I'd had a son like you.

PORFIRIO (*Giving him an unpleasant look*.): Yeah . . . Where were we?

DON PEDRO (*Animated*.): We were speaking about the assault on the presidential palace . . . Will there be any risk? Will it really be dangerous?

PORFIRIO (*Sullenly*.): You can never tell. Rosales commands a regiment of fifteen men—all armed. If even one of those imbeciles has cartridges of the same calibre as his gun, we can expect the worst. Should he so much as blind one of my followers in one eye firing at random out the window, history will stick the word "butcher" in front of my name. Like that poor old Lopez Lopez y Macaña who lost a man during a scuffle . . .

DON PEDRO: A stray bullet?

PORFIRIO: Not even that. The fellow, drunk as a lord, was killed when he fell from the third floor of the palace. The newspapers immediately came out with horror stories. Foreign governments became concerned. Everywhere Lopez was called the ogre or the butcher. At night his opponents would come and sing the song "The Cruel Matador" under his window. It was just too much. He had to resign.

DON PEDRO: Dreadful!

PORFIRIO: No, we must avoid a bloody assault. Besides, I find the sight of blood very disagreeable. Just imagine the public square covered with corpses, blood flowing in the gutters, wailing widows, orphans calling for their fathers, and so forth, and so forth.

DON PEDRO: You're right. The best thing would be to hasten the voluntary resignation of Rosales.

PORFIRIO: It's easy to say, but that's the whole problem.

DON PEDRO: I think it would be better to proceed according to the old rules.

PORFIRIO: That is to say?

DON PEDRO: Attack with gold sovereigns!

PORFIRIO: How well I know.

DON PEDRO: Why not make an offer of twenty thousand pesos to Rosales?

PORFIRIO: You think that would be enough?

DON PEDRO: It's an enormous sum.

PORFIRIO: You think he'd accept?

DON PEDRO: I'm sure of it!

PORFIRIO: Of course, this would save time as well as lives. Thank you for your idea. The revolution will give full recognition for your services. We'll send an emissary to Rosales. Go get the required sum.

DON PEDRO (*Suffocated.*): But sir, how do you expect me to come by twenty thousand pesos?

PORFIRIO: Please continue addressing me as Excellency!

DON PEDRO: But, Excellency, twenty thousand pesos is a fabulous fortune!

PORFIRIO: Exactly. And I don't possess even the beginnings of such a sum. But you, dear friend . . . very dear friend, very very very dear . . .

DON PEDRO: I'm as poor as . . .

PORFIRIO: . . . as Job. You've already said that.

DON PEDRO (*Panicky.*): You couldn't have believed what my poor wife . . .

PORFIRIO: Perhaps we could make a brief stop by that famous strongbox you prefer to the charms of your good spouse . . .

VOICE OF BOMBITA (*Crying out as loud as he can.*): One million, two million, three million, four million, five million, six million . . .

PORFIRIO: Him again! He's gone back to his perch.

DON PEDRO: But the strongbox is empty, completely empty. It's never been used. All you'll see in it is a big spider web . . . a very ordinary spider web. No originality. It's not even worth going out of your way to see.

PORFIRIO: Let's go see it just the same.

VOICE OF BOMBITA [*Still crying out.*]: Ten thousand pesos, fifteen thousand pesos, twenty thousand pesos, thirty thousand pesos, a hundred thousand pesos! . . .

PORFIRIO: Good God, the nasty devil knows how to count!

DON PEDRO [*Furious, he runs toward the door.*]: Will you shut up, you dirty little beast!

VOICE OF BOMBITA: Do you want to see the condition of my bottom? Do you want to see the condition of my bottom? . . . One million, two million, three million, four million, five million! . . .

PORFIRIO [*Amused.*]: You go first. I'll follow . . .

DON PEDRO: No, no, I mean, if I turn that sum over to you, I'm completely ruined. I won't have anything left! I'll be as bad off as a lowly worm!

PORFIRIO: Why, we're only talking about a loan.

DON PEDRO: What do you mean, a loan?

PORFIRIO: I'll sign a receipt redeemable by the state treasury.

DON PEDRO: But the state treasury is empty!

PORFIRIO: I'll fill it up again.

DON PEDRO: There's nothing left to sell. Your predecessors sold everything to the banana trusts: railroads, telephone company, everything!

PORFIRIO: I beg your pardon! My proposal to the Star Company was that if they backed my candidacy and paid my troops for a week, I would sell them, as co-owners, the ground floor of the presidential palace.

DON PEDRO [*Flabbergasted.*]: The ground fl . . . And they accepted?

PORFIRIO: You bet they did! It'll make a wonderful banana warehouse.

DON PEDRO [*Interested.*]: And how much will you make?

PORFIRIO: The state will gain 100,000 pesos.

DON PEDRO: My goodness!

PORFIRIO: Do you want to see the contract?

DON PEDRO: No, no.

PORFIRIO: What's bothering you then?

DON PEDRO: Nothing, nothing. I was just thinking that for a structure built of stone, an historical monument, in short . . .

PORFIRIO: Oh, the Star Company doesn't give a damn about the twenty years of glory of that old-fashioned palace. They bought it because of its thick wall, because the interior is cool.

DON PEDRO (*Pained.*): Exactly. It seems to me 100,000 pesos is very little.

PORFIRIO: Really?

DON PEDRO: You could have asked twice as much.

PORFIRIO: I don't have a good business head. Besides, I don't think they'd have gone along. So, as soon as I'm in office I'm paid 100,000 pesos, and I reimburse you your money.

DON PEDRO: And the interest?

PORFIRIO: What interest?

DON PEDRO: What do you think? If I lend you twenty thousand pesos, it's only right I make something out of the transaction!

PORFIRIO: Now look here. It seems to me you're trying to speculate on our freedom-revolution. What if I had you shot?

DON PEDRO: Don't do that! . . . Let's assume I said nothing!

PORFIRIO: Go get the money for me right away!

DON PEDRO: Couldn't we offer the infamous Rosales only ten thousand pesos?

PORFIRIO: He'd never accept. It's too little. If I were in his place, I'd refuse.

DON PEDRO: We could try.

PORFIRIO (*Tired.*): Let's try then.

SCENE 4

The same plus Juanita and a soldier.

DON PEDRO: Oh! My lord!

PORFIRIO: Now what?

DON PEDRO: My daughter!

THE SOLDIER: General, I just found this young lady while searching the house.

JUANITA (*Struggling furiously.*): Let go of me! Let go of me! You brute! *She slaps the soldier.*

DON PEDRO (*At his wits end.*): That's my daughter! Don't touch her!

JUANITA: Let go of me you idiot. Your hands are filthy and you smell bad!

PORFIRIO (*To the soldier.*): All right. Let her alone.

JUANITA: I was just doing some embroidery when this character came into my room without knocking. How despicable!

THE SOLDIER: She hit me. She's a plucky bitch!

DON PEDRO: That's my youngest daughter and she wouldn't hurt anybody.

THE SOLDIER: Wouldn't hurt anybody? She came at me like a tornado and threatened to put my eyes out with her pair of scissors! . . . Sir, you promised us this wouldn't be a dangerous revolution and I almost had my eyes put out!

JUANITA: I was just embroidering this handkerchief. When he came in, I defended myself.

PORFIRIO: Let's see that handkerchief. Caramba! That's my name!

JUANITA: Are you General Porfirio?

PORFIRIO (*Touched.*): And you thought of the idea of embroidering "Long live Porfirio!" on this handkerchief?

JUANITA: I wanted to offer it to you.

PORFIRIO: An impulse of the moment! That reminds me of something . . . yes. Ah! Du Guesclin!

DON PEDRO: Who?

PORFIRIO: There's proof the people love me! The girls of my country embroider for me just as the girls of France used to spin yarn for Du Guesclin.

DON PEDRO: That was probably that French president who wore the collapsible top hat and leggings.

PORFIRIO (*To Juanita.*): Thank you my child. Thank you. I am very touched!

JUANITA (*Full of mischief.*): Oh, I can see that.

SCENE 5

The same, plus Manuel and the Second Soldier.

SECOND SOLDIER: Sir, I just found this man.

DON PEDRO: A man? In my house?

SECOND SOLDIER: I found him hiding behind the barrels in the cellar. He scared me out of my wits.

DON PEDRO: Damnation! It's Manuel. General, have him shot. Have him shot immediately!

SECOND SOLDIER: I was going to run, then I saw he wasn't offering any resistance.

DON PEDRO (*With uncontrollable rage.*): Have him shot . . . Seducer! Have him tied to the mouth of a cannon!

PORFIRIO: Silence! What were you doing in the cellar?

MANUEL: I am Juanita's fiancé.

DON PEDRO: That's a lie! That's disgraceful! That's not true, I swear it! . . . Shoot him! For pity's sake. Avenge the honor of a grievously offended father.

PORFIRIO: Stop howling like that.

JUANITA: Have pity, General! I love him.

DON PEDRO (*Beside himself.*): You good-for-nothing! Have them shot together! . . . No! I don't know what I'm saying any more. Ungrateful good-for-nothing. Making your old father suffer like that. You deserve to be shut up in a convent. Doña Cumacha said it would come to this. If I had whipped you, this would never have happened!

PORFIRIO: Will you ever shut up? You can't hear yourself talk with this old reptile. I want to clear up this business myself. Why were you hiding in the cellar?

SECOND SOLDIER: He was stretched out behind a keg reading by candle light.

DON PEDRO: By candle light? He's a witness. He wanted to set fire to the house! Have him shot as an arsonist!

VOICE OF BOMBITA: Have him shot! Have him shot! Have him shot! Have him shot!

PORFIRIO: That's enough. Shut up! Stop squawking like that. Damn it all, your splitting my ears . . .

DON PEDRO: It's the parrot.

PORFIRIO: No, it's you.

DON PEDRO: He wanted to blow us all up!

PORFIRIO: Manuel, tell me the truth. What were you doing in the cellar?

DON PEDRO: He's a counterrevolutionary! Shoot him, please. He made a bomb to get you—to get us all. I'm sure of it.

PORFIRIO: Don Pedro, if you keep him from talking once more, I'll have you gagged! And your parrot too! Manuel, what were you doing in that cellar? Don Pedro, don't open your mouth or I'll hit you over the head.

MANUEL: I can't tell you.

DON PEDRO: You see! An assassination attempt! He was preparing to kill us. He's one of those horrible terrorists. We were almost blown up! He's being paid by Rosales. We have escaped an assassination attempt. Murderer!

VOICE OF BOMBITA: Murderer! soldier! pig! One million, two million, three million, four million, five million, six million!

PORFIRIO (*Holding his head.*): It's enough to drive you crazy! . . . Don Pedro, one more word and I'll pull out all your feathers! . . . Oh . . . I don't know what I'm saying! . . . (*To Manuel.*) My boy, you've got to tell me everything!

MANUEL (*Firmly.*): I won't talk.

PORFIRIO: Ha!

DON PEDRO (*Triumphantly.*): You see!

PORFIRIO: Too bad. Shoot him.

SECOND SOLDIER: We don't have any more cartridges, sir!

PORFIRIO: That does it! What a mess. How do you expect me to get myself out of this one?

DON PEDRO: Hang him! I'll furnish the rope at two pesos a yard.

JUANITA: I'll tell you everything!

PORFIRIO: Finally.

JUANITA: Manuel was waiting for nightfall.

PORFIRIO (*Mopping his brow.*): To do what?

JUANITA: To run off with me.

DON PEDRO: Damn it all. The things I have to listen to at my age. Scoundrel! He was going to abduct my beloved daughter and dishonor her!

PORFIRIO (*To Juanita.*): Go on!

JUANITA: Using the revolution, your revolution, as a cover, Manuel was supposed to run off with me tonight!

PORFIRIO: That explains the handkerchief?

JUANITA: Euh . . . yes. And tomorrow morning we were to be married.

DON PEDRO: You can't. I oppose this marriage!

VOICE OF BOMBITA: Have him shot! Have him shot! Have him shot! One banana, two bananas, three bananas, four bananas, five bananas, six bananas . . . Fifteen thousand pesos, twenty thousand pesos, a hundred thousand pesos!

PORFIRIO: Ah, that one! (*To Don Pedro.*) Why are you against the union? These young people love one another.

DON PEDRO: She's too young. She's only eighteen, and I still need her around here. Besides, I can't give her a dowry.

MANUEL: I don't want one.

DON PEDRO: Hmm . . . You would take her like this? Naked?

MANUEL: Leave her at least what she's wearing!

DON PEDRO (*Shrugging his shoulders.*): It's just a way of talking.

MANUEL: Do we agree?

DON PEDRO: Hold on, hold on. Not so fast, young man! I have just been wronged. My honor has been trifled with. Wouldn't your father, Don Enrique, be willing to cancel a debt I contracted with him some years ago by way of compensation?

MANUEL: Of course.

DON PEDRO: You are witnesses. He accepts my daughter just as she is and I no longer owe his father anything!

Manuel and Juanita rush into one another's arms.

PORFIRIO: Well, that was handled with dispatch. Manuel, I'm going to offer you a wedding present. I'm making you a general. You know how to read and write and you have shoes! . . .

MANUEL (*With Juanita leaning against him.*): If I have a choice, I'd prefer to be an admiral.

PORFIRIO (*Regally.*): Granted. Naturally the purchase of a uniform and cap are at your own expense.

JUANITA: Oh my darling, how handsome you're going to be as a sailor!

DON PEDRO (*Bitter.*): I would like to respectfully remind His Excellency that we are going to have an admiral, but we don't have a navy.

PORFIRIO (*Between Don Pedro and Manuel.*): That's right, Manuel. We don't have a navy.

MANUEL: Is that all? Our forests are big enough. We'll build one.

PORFIRIO (*To Don Pedro.*): He says we'll build one.

DON PEDRO: Perhaps. But how are we going to sail our ships—we're a landlocked country?

PORFIRIO (*To Manuel.*): He says our country is landlocked.

MANUEL: We'll build a river flotilla!

PORFIRIO: He says we'll build a river flotilla.

DON PEDRO (*Sarcastically.*): But we don't have a river and the only stream we have isn't deep enough to sail a canoe.

PORFIRIO: That's true.

MANUEL: We don't have a river? We'll create one later! You don't think this is the first time a government has named an official and come up with the tangible reasons for his appointment later?

PORFIRIO: He's right. Besides, I've had enough of this. Manuel, I'm entrusting you with a most urgent and important mission.

MANUEL: I'm listening.

PORFIRIO: Your father-in-law is going to turn over to you ten thousand pesos . . .

MANUEL: A miracle!

PORFIRIO: . . . that you will go propose to Rosales as an inducement for his immediate resignation.

MANUEL: I understand.

PORFIRIO: I'm giving you twenty minutes; be as eloquent as you can!

MANUEL: I will.

PORFIRIO: Be persuasive!

MANUEL: Count on me.

PORFIRIO: The fate of the Revolution is in your hands. And what a revolution! When General Félix implements his ten-year plan, you'll see! No one will have anything to do but take it easy. Félix will think for everyone. A golden age! Don Pedro, go turn over the ten thousand pesos to him.

JUANITA (*To Manuel.*): I'm going with you.

PORFIRIO: There's not one second to lose.

MANUEL: We're on our way.

PORFIRIO: Don Pedro, don't look so glum. You'll get your ten thousand pesos back.

Both exit.

SCENE 6

Porfirio, Gamello. Gamello has burst in with his bomb under his arm at the very moment of Manuel's exit. His eyes are gleaming. Excitedly.

GAMELLO: Chief! Chief! I've done it! It's set! I've found the detonator! Can we go ahead now?

PORFIRIO: We'll have to wait a little. I've just opened negotiations.

GAMELLO (*Despairing.*): Negotiations! Why it could go off at any time! Twelve years of research! Chief, please let me go see Rosales!

PORFIRIO: I can't consider it. I'll have to have an answer from Rosales!

GAMELLO (*More and more excited.*): Just listen to it! . . . (*He brings the device close to Porfirio's ear.*) It's set I tell you!

PORFIRIO (*Solemnly.*): I don't hear anything! . . . . Ah, yes! The ticking of an alarm clock.

GAMELLO (*Glowing.*): Eh? Just what I'm telling you! In a few minutes, bababoom!

VOICE OF BOMBITA: Bababoom!

GAMELLO (*With a start.*): Good God! . . . No, it can't be her!

The First Soldier comes in with Marifé.

SCENE 7

Porfirio, Gamello, Marifé, First Soldier.

PORFIRIO (*To Gamello.*): Leave me now! Go over to the palace and await my orders!

Gamello leaves clutching the bomb in his arms while Porfirio, with a wonderstruck gaze, watches Marifé approach.

FIRST SOLDIER: Sir, I found this in the kitchen.

PORFIRIO: Was she embroidering a handkerchief?

FIRST SOLDIER: No, she was peeling potatoes. She's kicked me in the shins so much I won't be able to walk for a week. I'm going on sick call tonight, sir.

PORFIRIO: All right. . . . Now go look for her boyfriend! If he isn't in the cellar, try the stables!

The soldier hobbles out.

SCENE 8

Porfirio, Marifé.

PORFIRIO: Pretty as you are, you must have a boyfriend.

MARIFÉ (*Haughtily.*): That's no business of yours.

PORFIRIO: Wait a minute. Do you know who you're talking to?

MARIFÉ: Your thug of a uniformed bodyguard told me. Is that supposed to mean something to me?

PORFIRIO (*To himself.*): Adorable creature!

MARIFÉ (*Curtly.*): I don't think we have anything to say to one another! Now let me leave!

PORFIRIO: One minute! Did anyone ever tell you you're pretty enough to make a stone smile?

MARIFÉ (*Offended.*): Sir!

PORFIRIO: Is it a crime to say that the mere sight of you makes my heart skip a beat? It was a big shock for me!

He tries to take her hand.

MARIFÉ: Don't touch me!

PORFIRIO: Is it wrong to tell you I've never seen such a charming face and that Nature is . . .

MARIFÉ: I'm not listening to you.

She makes as if to leave.

PORFIRIO: Don't be cruel. Stay another minute. Do I frighten you?

MARIFÉ: I don't want to stay one minute more. I am a decent girl!

PORFIRIO: I can certainly see that. . . . (*He sighs.*) Why don't you want to love me the way I love you?

MARIFÉ: You get down to work fast! (*She defends herself against him.*) I'm going to have to . . . (*She slaps him.*) There! It's your fault . . .

PORFIRIO: You break my heart.

MARIFÉ: I'm probably not the first.

PORFIRIO: Don't make fun of me! I'm hooked. A fire has been burning inside me since you came in here.

MARIFÉ: Don't come near me or I'll scream.

PORFIRIO: My darling, my little dove . . .

Slowly he comes near Marifé, speaking to her in a soft voice, while she remains on her guard.

SCENE 9

The same, plus First Soldier, Manuel, Gamello, and Félix who come in by turns.

FIRST SOLDIER: General, I couldn't find the boyfriend. There's only a mule in the stable. I said to myself, that's not him, so . . .

Porfirio makes a gesture of impatience. The soldier disappears. At the same moment Manuel appears.

MANUEL: Chief! Chief! Rosales signed! Quick, quick, to the palace!

PORFIRIO (*Impatient.*): Leave me alone.

MANUEL: Rosales agreed to sign the resignation statement. But we shouldn't leave the presidential chair vacant very long. That would be dangerous.

An angry gesture from Porfirio and he disappears. Félix comes in busy-looking. He throws a big suitcase on the table and hangs a sign on the wall: "Be brief. Our time is more valuable than yours!"

FÉLIX: Chief, the big day is here. Fifteen years of perfecting it! An incomparable card index file! Everything is ready. (*He opens the suitcase.*) But you must hurry!

Gamello comes in with his bomb.

GAMELLO: Quick, quick! There's not a second to lose Chief! Ah, Chief, the Revolution is victorious! I didn't have to use my bomb. I'm keeping it for the next one.

PORFIRIO (*Wrenched away from his flirtation.*): What are you saying?

GAMELLO: You must get over to the palace quickly!

PORFIRIO: What's going on?

FÉLIX: Rosales has left. It's yours! yours! Quick! Quick!

PORFIRIO (*Resigned.*): Good. Very well. I'm coming (*To Marifé.*) Goodbye, my little wild flower! Duty calls me . . . Goodbye. Goodbye.

In the street the crowd is chanting: "Porfirio! Porfirio!

PORFIRIO: But my heart remains here!

Marifé turns her back to him sulkily. Porfirio opens the window and mournfully listens to the mounting acclamations as the curtain falls.

END OF THE SECOND ACT

ACT THREE

SCENE 1

Porfirio, Félix. As the curtain goes up, Félix is arranging his file cards. Porfirio, very nervous, comes in. He glances at his portrait hung in the very place where Rosales's had been. He then goes to listen at the door at the back. Félix watches him on the sly.

PORFIRIO (*Thinking of other things.*): Well, is everything going the way you wanted?

FÉLIX: Not bad. In one week the whole population has signed the form in accordance with the law on compulsory happiness. I'm waiting for the results from the rural areas, but the capital's two thousand residents have declared themselves happy under the new regime.

PORFIRIO (*As before.*): It's a big success.

FÉLIX: Yes, but there were a few unexpected occurrences.

PORFIRIO: For example?

FÉLIX: General Papagayo had just learned an hour beforehand that his wife had been playing around outrageously on him and that he wasn't the father of his five children.

PORFIRIO: Did he sign?

FÉLIX: He signed . . . People are a mystery! Just as Don Pedro signed, though he never did get back his ten thousand pesos. I only have one refusal to complain about. Obviously that can't justify the opening of a reeducation camp.

PORFIRIO: Who is it?

FÉLIX: Marifé! . . . Just the whim of an overly spoiled child.

PORFIRIO: Are you sure?

FÉLIX: Eh! She was in this very room trying to show she has a mind of her own. I won't even talk about one other case which is . . . how shall I put it? . . . more delicate.

PORFIRIO (*Violent.*): I couldn't sign! I'm not happy, that's all.

FÉLIX: Perhaps. Perhaps. But can't you see what kind of a situation you're putting me in? If the reporters got hold of that? The Republic's highest official not conforming with one of the basic laws of the new State. That's enough to disturb thinking, baffle good will, upset minds, spread confusion among the populace, and encourage malcontents!

PORFIRIO (*Tired.*): Take care of it as best you can.

FÉLIX: It's going to be difficult.

PORFIRIO: Do you think she'll come?

FÉLIX: Who's that?

PORFIRIO: Marifé!

FÉLIX: Where?

PORFIRIO: To the ball. The ball is going to begin in the public square in a few minutes. It's an idea I had this morning. A compulsory public ball. The police will be searching the houses. She'll have to leave her room.

FÉLIX: Perhaps this girl loves another man.

PORFIRIO: You're crazy!

FÉLIX: We can always look at her record card . . . Fifteen years of research. The only file system of its kind in the world. The life of every citizen of the Republic is carefully recorded in it.

PORFIRIO: All right, all right! Hurry up and look!

FÉLIX (*Looking.*): M . . . M . . . M . . . M . . . M . . . Ma . . . Ma . . . Mari . . . Marif . . . Marifé! Here we are . . . Untouched!

PORFIRIO: Her file card?

FÉLIX: The girl herself also.

PORFIRIO: Go on, go on!

FÉLIX: Beauty spot on her left shoulder blade. Twenty-one years of age . . . Never wears a brassiere . . . Rides a bicycle . . . Stubborn as a mule . . . Loves honey cakes . . .

PORFIRIO: That's all?

FÉLIX: No boyfriends.

PORFIRIO: Ah!

FÉLIX: Yes, but this information is already one month old. In one week a girl can . . .

PORFIRIO: Quiet, idiot!

FÉLIX (*Vehement.*): Listen Chief. I'm telling you, this isn't the time to be thinking of nonsense. The ten-year plan has been in effect six days and here you are feeling dejected over a silly little girl.

PORFIRIO: What are you complaining about? I've authorized you to set up your ministry in this house. I've doubled the size of the police force. You have permission to use as you see fit the presses of the national printing office. And God only knows they're always running! In six days the walls of the whole town have been covered with posters, the official newspaper has had to be doubled in size to take care of all the new decrees.

FÉLIX: All which goes to prove that it's lucky I'm here.

PORFIRIO: Our citizens spend all their time filling out questionnaires, signing forms, and standing in line in front of the new offices you've set up.

FÉLIX: Before we had anarchy! Now we have order. No more lack of direction. No more improvising. No more whims. A clock! Each citizen will be a well-regulated clock.

PORFIRIO: Really? . . . At any rate, the ball is going to begin. You'll see to it that everyone in this house attends.

FÉLIX: I understand. Count on me.

Porfirio exits.

FÉLIX (*Toward the wings.*): Next!

SCENE 2

Félix. The Gentleman in Gray.

THE GENTLEMAN IN GRAY: It's to renew my card for using pedestrian crosswalks to cross the street.

FÉLIX: Let's see that card.

THE GENTLEMAN IN GRAY: I also wanted to ask . . . This card authorizes me to use fifty pedestrian crosswalks per week. But just to come here to renew my card I have to use seventeen crosswalks.

FÉLIX: I can't do anything about that.

THE GENTLEMAN IN GRAY: And the worst of it is I live across the street from my office. When I run out of tickets I have to go three miles to find a path that will take me back to the sidewalk across the street from my house! It's absurd.

FÉLIX (*Very curt.*): It's the law!

THE GENTLEMAN IN GRAY: The law, the law! The people who make them travel around in cars!

FÉLIX (*Threatening.*): I will request you to watch what you say. I'm going to put that remark down on your card.

THE GENTLEMAN IN GRAY: Excuse me!

FÉLIX: You know the penalty? Treasonable talk can get you from about six months to thirty or forty years in prison.

THE GENTLEMAN IN GRAY: I'm not looking for trouble. I didn't say anything.

FÉLIX: Here's your card. Now go to Office 78 for your tickets and then to the Traffic Office for their stamp. After that you'll have to go to the Highway Department for registration.

THE GENTLEMAN IN GRAY: This little operation is going to take another hour of my time.

FÉLIX: All you think of is complaining, my good man . . . Wait! Let's take a look at your file . . . (*He takes out the file.*) Well, well, well, well!

THE GENTLEMAN IN GRAY (*Concerned.*): Is it serious?

FÉLIX: I read here in red letters . . .

THE GENTLEMAN IN GRAY (*Same as before.*): In red letters? . . .

FÉLIX: At the beginning of Topo y Topo's presidency you distinctly shouted—and this is confirmed by two witnesses—"Down with softies!"

THE GENTLEMAN IN GRAY: Me! I shouted that? . . . I don't remember it!

FÉLIX: I know, I know. They never remember. Words evaporate in the air. At least that's what they think . . . But I stayed on the alert and you can't deny . . . You shouted, "Down with softies!"

THE GENTLEMAN IN GRAY (*Stuttering.*): It's possible . . . but . . .

FÉLIX: There are no buts! In short you're one of these dissatisfied malcontents who are against everything.

THE GENTLEMAN IN GRAY: Me?

FÉLIX: I'll keep an eye on you, my good man.

THE GENTLEMAN IN GRAY (*Suddenly brightening up.*): But at the time of General Topo y topo I was scarcely six years old!

FÉLIX: Are you sure?

THE GENTLEMAN IN GRAY: Check the dates yourself.

FÉLIX: My gosh that's right! But that doesn't change the seriousness of the case. It was a cry of treason! On the contrary that proves a serious precocity . . . Now get out of here! But I won't forget you.

Bent over and bewildered looking, the Gentleman in Gray leaves rolling his eyes.

SCENE 3

Félix, Gamello.

GAMELLO (*He comes in running with his bomb still under his arm.*): Ah, good friend! Porfirio is asking if the girl is ready for the ball. He has really fallen for her. Where is she?

FÉLIX: I don't know anything about that. I'm working. I'm not interested in hearing about making out with the opposite sex, I'm thinking about the government.

GAMELLO (*Interested.*): All right. That bat in your belfry isn't doing any better!

FÉLIX (*Irritated.*): By the way, what about your bomb.

GAMELLO: You too! . . . How humiliating! . . . You know very well Porfirio got Rosales to resign of his own volition. If he hadn't, I'd have blown him up, blooey! Like that!

He sets his bomb down on Félix's table. The latter knocks it off with a careless gesture.

FÉLIX: Put that somewhere else. You're going to get my papers dirty!

GAMELLO: You're crazy! If it had gone off! . . .

He picks it up and listens to the mechanism.

FÉLIX: Come now. It's as harmless as a chamber pot!

GAMELLO (*Indignant.*): My bomb may look like a chamber pot, but your revolution is beginning to give us all a belly ache!

FÉLIX (*Very dignified.*): Leave me! Go tell Porfirio I shall personally take care of his little ostrich.

GAMELLO: I prefer that. Good evening.

He leaves at a gallop.

SCENE 4

Félix. The Lady in Pink. Félix, to the wings: "Next." The Lady in Pink comes in.

FÉLIX (*Arrogantly.*): My respects, Madam. Now what is it about? Let's hurry along!

THE LADY IN PINK: It's about having a baby.

FÉLIX (*Flabbergasted.*): What?

THE LADY IN PINK: Well. I want to do things in accordance with the Planned Parenthood Program!

FÉLIX: Ah, of course. Are you legally married?

THE LADY IN PINK: Yes sir. I turned twenty-one the day before yesterday and, in keeping with the law, I chose a husband among the three individuals whose pictures the civil status supervisor put in front of me along with their names, professions and details on their temperament. I chose the young man whose data card reads: Jealous and rather vigorous.

FÉLIX: My compliments, Madam. In how much time do you want to have this child?

THE LADY IN PINK (*At a loss.*): Oh, as soon as possible! I mean, I wouldn't want to be late and get in trouble with the Planned Parenthood supervisor.

FÉLIX: I fully understand. Let's see . . . Our Planned Parenthood program provides for five hundred births a month . . . Wait a minute . . . (*He consults a register.*) The months of March, April and May of next year are filled up.

THE LADY IN PINK: Oh!

FÉLIX: You'll have to . . . That's it, you'll have to wait three months and two days to have the authorization to begin this child, if you understand what I mean.

THE LADY IN PINK (*Same as before.*): Yes, yes . . . Could you set a day for me?

FÉLIX: That's not my section. Go to the Planned Parenthood Department and fill out a form in six copies. Answer questionnaire 11-A . . . Then we'll see.

THE LADY IN PINK: All right . . . Thank you.

FÉLIX (*Friendly.*): At your service, dear lady. Oof! What a day! And now we're going to have a dance . . . That Porfirio is a jackass!
Marifé comes in.

SCENE 5

Félix, Marifé.

FÉLIX: Ah! Young lady! I should tell you . . . Attendance at the dance in a little while is compulsory.

MARIFÉ: I'm not going.

FÉLIX: Oh ho! Refusal to obey . . . I would also like to point out to you that, as you'll turn twenty-one in a month, you'll have to think about getting married.

MARIFÉ: I will never get married!

FÉLIX: They say that. But the law's the law; you'll have to obey it!

MARIFÉ: I prefer to go to jail.

FÉLIX: Nonsense.

MARIFÉ: I'm too unhappy.

FÉLIX: That's against regulations!

MARIFÉ: What do I care about regulations!

FÉLIX: I'm a patient man, young lady, but watch what you say! We talk and we talk without paying much attention to what we say. Then, one fine day someone confronts us with remarks we made in careless moments, and we are nabbed by the law's long arm. And that'll get you from six months to twenty years or more!

Marifé shrugs her shoulders.

FÉLIX: Are you coming then?

MARIFÉ: No.

FÉLIX: Very well. I'm going to make my report. I'll have you waltzing, young lady! I've put more whimsical people than you in their place.

He goes out taking his files and his suitcase full of file cards. As soon as he has left he is heard shouting to the line of people waiting: "That's all for today! Come back tomorrow: The window is closed! Assemble for festivities on the square!"

SCENE 6

Marifé, Don Pedro, Doña Cumacha. The latter are all dressed up to go to the ball.

DOÑA CUMACHA: Let's hurry! Let's hurry! They're going to call roll.

DON PEDRO: My dear, let me catch my breath!

DOÑA CUMACHA: Marifé! You miserable girl. You're not ready yet? Do you want to get us in trouble with the Office of Public Festivities?

DON PEDRO: I'm giving you one minute to get ready!

MARIFÉ (*Ready to cry.*): I'm not going to the ball. I'm not going to the ball!

DOÑA CUMACHA: You'll see, Don Pedro, this bull-headed girl will cause us a night in jail.

DON PEDRO: Let me ask her some questions in peace. (*To Marifé.*) Now why don't you want to come? I mean it's senseless . . . What reasons can you give us?

DOÑA CUMACHA: Your father is letting you go out for once; you'd do well to take advantage of it! It's a unique opportunity that perhaps won't occur again, except in the unexpected case of your getting married.

DON PEDRO: Come now daughter.

MARIFÉ (*Stubborn.*): I prefer to stay home. Now that General Félix is gone I won't be bothered.

DON PEDRO: Tell me the truth. Did General Porfirio misbehave with you?

MARIFÉ: Of course not!

DOÑA CUMACHA: Did he make overtures to you?

MARIFÉ: Yes.

DOÑA CUMACHA: And you were offended?

MARIFÉ: Yes.

DON PEDRO: At least, I hope you didn't slap him.

MARIFÉ: Uh . . . no.

DON PEDRO: That's a relief.

DOÑA CUMACHA (*Slyly.*): Did he take you in his arms?

MARIFÉ: Auntie! Are you crazy? I'd never allow . . .

DON PEDRO: Doña Cumacha, mind your own business. (*To Marifé.*) If President Porfirio wasn't offensive, but simply gallant and attentive, why refuse his invitation? . . . Because, after all, it appears to be because of you that he's giving this ball.

MARIFÉ: What do I care?

DOÑA CUMACHA: Oh! How fresh!

MARIFÉ (*Exasperated.*): I don't like to dance. There! I don't like having a man holding me in his arms. Does that satisfy you?

DON PEDRO: If that's all it is, you should overcome your disgust all the same, at least in your father's interest.

MARIFÉ: What do you mean, in my father's interest?

DON PEDRO (*Whimpering.*): The fact is this fiend has borrowed a fortune from me. I'm ruined if he doesn't give me back the ten thousand pesos I had to lend him! It'll be the death of me, dear Marifé, you who are so sweet to your old papa! And our general-president could take revenge on me for the snubs of my darling daughter. Do you understand, my little dove?

MARIFÉ: So, father, you'd have preferred that I let him embrace me the other day so you wouldn't fear his being against you now? But only because you don't want to lose your miserable pesos! You put a very low price on the honor and reputation of your daughter.

DON PEDRO: But I never said that.

DOÑA CUMACHA: That's about what your remarks add up to!

DON PEDRO: You be quiet! Now, my dear daughter! I am an old man. That monster could avenge your proud attitude by refusing to return the huge sum he got out of me . . . Come now, darling! All you'd have to do is to go to the ball and, bless my soul, while dancing with this individual, who isn't nearly as repulsive as they say, drop a word in your conversation reminding him of his little debt, just like that, without being obvious . . . Who knows? He might even turn the money over to you . . . Then you could leave him and come back to me, since you dislike him so much.

MARIFÉ: Father, if I go to that ball, I won't ask that tin soldier for anything, for I'd refuse to dance with him.

DON PEDRO (*Furious.*): And what does this mean? You are foolish and stubborn and you don't love your father!

MARIFÉ (*Same tone.*): Father, I'm surprised at you. After having locked me up in this house for twenty years so that my virtue wouldn't be the slightest bit tarnished, after keeping me away from the windows facing the courtyard and the street, you can come here and reproach me for not being flirtatious enough with a man I detest!

DON PEDRO: What's all that speech about? You'll go to the ball if I order you to! And, moreover, I don't want to have any trouble with the authorities!

MARIFÉ: If you make me go, I'll tell everyone what my father is demanding of me, that he wants me to be nice with the General-President in order to . . .

DON PEDRO: Enough! You ungrateful girl!

He goes to slap her.

DOÑA CUMACHA: That's it . . . Let me tell that good-looking Porfirio you mistreat his ladylove and he'll have you shot!

DON PEDRO (*Turning on her.*): You! You'll get yours too! These women are driving me crazy!

DOÑA CUMACHA: You've been that way for a long time . . .

DON PEDRO: What! You dare? . . .

SCENE 7

Marifé, Don Pedro, Doña Cumacha, Juanita.

JUANITA: Father, I'm glad to find you here. General Porfirio just gave me these ten thousand pesos to bring back to you.

DON PEDRO: I'm dreaming . . . (*He opens the envelope.*) All there! All of them! Ten thousand in peso notes! . . . Like little yellow chicks! . . . My dear little ones! . . . (*He kisses the envelope.*) Well! I'm going to thank him right away.

JUANITA: That's it! Leave us alone for awhile!

DOÑA CUMACHA: You've become very bossy since you've gotten married! . . .

DON PEDRO: You've probably some important things to say to your sister?

JUANITA: That's exactly right! . . . But I don't want you to hear any of it.

DON PEDRO: Very well! Very well! We're leaving! Doña Cumacha, come with me . . . Let's go.

DOÑA CUMACHA: I'm dying to know what they'll say to each other.

DON PEDRO (*Leading her away.*): Come on, come on! I'm going to dance with you my dear! This envelope has given me wings! You'll see! You will fly away in my arms!

They exit.

SCENE 8

Marifé, Juanita.

JUANITA: Why do you refuse to go to the dance? It's a big success and they're having a good time. I can swear to it.

MARIFÉ: It's all the same to me.

JUANITA: You should see Porfirio.

MARIFÉ: What do I care about what he's doing.

JUANITA: He's surrounded by the prettiest girls in the capital.

MARIFÉ: You didn't come running over here and get rid of our parents just to tell me that trivia . . . Why, then?

JUANITA: Well, it's because Porfirio is as sad as a rusty saber. And he's getting thin and yellow since he's been in power.

MARIFÉ: If affairs of state cause him so much worry, all he has to do is resign! . . . Thank God, we're not lacking in generals to serve as a successor!

JUANITA: To come to the point, Marifé, don't play dumb! . . . You know he's madly in love with you! Don't tell me you're not aware of the situation! What's more, he wants to come for you here . . .

MARIFÉ: Here? What does he take me for? And by what right? . . . I'm completely fed up! . . . If he should dare . . .

JUANITA: That's just it! He doesn't dare!

MARIFÉ: Did he tell you so?

JUANITA: That's what he told Manuel who repeated it to me with the advice to get you prepared for the visit!

MARIFÉ: A fine state of affairs! A fine profession you've picked up for yourself . . . Well I'll put him out, you'll see!

JUANITA: But, darling, I just came to get your opinion! If you find him that repulsive, I'll let Manuel know. That way he can warn him and get him to drop that idea!

MARIFÉ: I didn't say that! I don't find him repulsive!

JUANITA: If you love someone else or if you don't like Porfirio's paying special attention to you, let me know right now!

MARIFÉ: That's not the case!

JUANITA: If you want the State to find a husband for you at age twenty-one, through regular channels as the law provides, that's up to you! . . .

MARIFÉ: That's something else completely!

JUANITA: Am I to inform him he should in no case come and that he should leave you alone for good?

MARIFÉ: You're distorting my point of view.

JUANITA: Anyway . . . here he is! I'm going back to the dance and to Manuel. You can tell Porfirio yourself that you hate him, you despise him and the very sight of him makes you sick, that you would prefer to marry Gamello . . . in short, anything you want . . . Good bye!

She leaves.

MARIFÉ: Don't leave me alone! . . .

But Porfirio has already taken her place.

SCENE 9

Porfirio, Marifé

PORFIRIO: My darling, you have before you the most powerful man in the Republic and also the most unhappy one.

MARIFÉ: I thought nothing could match the charms of absolute power.

PORFIRIO: How beautiful you are! . . . Ah! I would like . . .

MARIFÉ: I don't know why you left the ball and all those beautiful accommodating women you had around. I can't understand your leaving so much merrymaking and music to come shut yourself up in this big sad house.

PORFIRIO: My darling, don't close me out! My life, my honor and my glory are at your feet, along with my heart! . . .

MARIFÉ: Yours is a heart that has given a great deal of service. You must give it often.

PORFIRIO: Slander! It's like new. If you were to take it in your hands, it would burn you, it would set you aflame from head to toe! . . .

MARIFÉ: Go away, please! It's not proper for a gentleman to stand so close to a girl!

PORFIRIO: I've offended you, my pet, my pearl, my little white carnation! Alongside you I am dirt! Mud! . . . Say the word and I'll go out that door! Put me out, if I have hurt you!

MARIFÉ: I will if you go too far.

PORFIRIO: Marifé, I love you and I want you to be mine! (*He takes her in his arms.*) Am I going too far? . . .

MARIFÉ: Umm! Almost!

PORFIRIO (*Lyrical.*): My love, just the word "yes" from your sweet lips and I'll be the happiest of men! . . . (*He holds her tightly in his arms.*) Am I going too far?

MARIFÉ: Oh my, I can't breathe!

PORFIRIO: Ah those lips that draw me and from which my soul could drink . . . (*He gives her a long kiss. Then, tenderly.*) Am I going too far?

MARIFÉ: I don't know . . . I think we have . . .

PORFIRIO: But you're not sure. Oh my sweetheart, my darling, my life!

MARIFÉ: Be careful, I hear someone coming!

Don Pedro comes in out of breath.

SCENE 10

Porfirio, Marifé. Don Pedro.

DON PEDRO: Damnation!

PORFIRIO (*Ill at ease.*): What's going on? Why so upset?

DON PEDRO: General, the fleet has revolted!

PORFIRIO: The fleet? . . . What fleet?

DON PEDRO: Why our fleet, the navy.

PORFIRIO: I don't understand.

DON PEDRO (*Getting his breath back.*): During your absence Admiral Manuel seized power.

PORFIRIO: Caramba! It's very clear that it's a put-up job. Manuel was the one who advised me to come here. The ungrateful traitor! . . . And he used you, Marifé! You were the bait, the lamb offered to the lion! . . . Unless . . . Oh, what a horrible suspicion!

MARIFÉ: Unless? . . . Come on, finish your sentence!

PORFIRIO: Unless you were an accomplice of that gangster. Come to think of it, we did rush things a bit awhile ago, eh baby?

MARIFÉ: An accomplice . . . Me?

PORFIRIO: Yes! The plot is childishly simple. Manuel advises me to come here to be with you. You agree to try to keep me, and during that time, bang! I'm thrown out!

DON PEDRO: Oh! General! That's absurd!

MARIFÉ: He's the one who took me in his arms! I wasn't after anything! . . . Oh! I hate him!

PORFIRIO: In short, I've had it again. Manuel has betrayed his benefactor, the person who facilitated his marriage. The person to whom he owes everything: happiness, honors, favors! . . . And to think I gave the order to build a motorboat in the botanical garden lagoon to justify his title of admiral of the fleet!

DON PEDRO: But you're wrong in suspecting my daughter! I tell you that before advising you to flee!

PORFIRIO: Flee?

DON PEDRO: Manuel has issued a warrant for your arrest.

PORFIRIO: That's the last straw . . . He's crazy. That's contrary to tradition! . . . And to think I was President of the Republic scarcely a week.

DON PEDRO: Just for the record, I'd like to point out that in 1923 General Patitas was in power less time than you.

PORFIRIO (*Watching the window.*): That seems hard to believe.

DON PEDRO: I beg your pardon. From the moment he signed the official register, went through the window, and landed on the sidewalk, eleven minutes and thirty seconds elapsed.

PORFIRIO: Didn't they arrest him?

DON PEDRO: Patitas? . . . They took him to the hospital.

PORFIRIO (*Shouting.*): There they are! They're coming! They won't take me alive! Give me a weapon! A skewer! A hammer! A pair of scissors! Anything! I will fight to the death!

MARIFÉ (*Horrified and admiringly.*): Porfirio! My darling! My love! My lion! . . .

PORFIRIO (*Who doesn't hear her.*): I'm going to transform this house into a fortress! They'll have to order an assault.

He walks back and forth furiously.

DON PEDRO: Not that! Stay calm! They don't want to harm you!

PORFIRIO: They won't take me alive . . . That rabble.

DON PEDRO: Everything is going to be straightened out. Calm down. It's only a dreadful misunderstanding.

MARIFÉ: He's exploding!

PORFIRIO: You, Don Pedro, stay by my side! You will die with me!

DON PEDRO: No General, no!

PORFIRIO (*Loudly.*): Too late. To arms!

DON PEDRO: I don't have any.

PORFIRIO: Scoundrel! Are you betraying me too? Betrayed by Manuel! Betrayed by the woman I adore! . . .

MARIFÉ: Porfirio! That's an ugly lie.

PORFIRIO: Betrayed by a disgraceful old man.

Don Pedro hurriedly takes the portrait of Porfirio from the wall and replaces it by one of Manuel.

MARIFÉ: Good heavens! They're coming up the stairs!

DON PEDRO: Remain calm, General. For the love of God, remain calm!

PORFIRIO (*Very excited.*): Don't shout like that! I am calm!

DON PEDRO (*Frantically.*): Let's be calm! Let's be calm!

SCENE 11

Porfirio, Don Pedro, Marifé, then Manuel. Manuel is wearing the cap of an admiral and is followed by the two soldiers dressed this time as sailors.

PORFIRIO (*In a rage.*): There's the traitor . . . Get a good look at him. See that hard look in his eye! that full lower lip so characteristic of people who kill their own brothers! . . . There's the man to put a dagger in your back! . . . Admiral of an aquarium! A ridiculous octopus! A sewer shark!

MANUEL: Shut up, you operetta general! I'll have you shot by a firing squad of sailors.

PORFIRIO: I am ready to die. Murderer. Butcher. Slaughterhouse pig sticker!

MANUEL: All right. Take hold of the tyrant and go shoot him. . . .

MARIFÉ (*Terrified.*): No! Manuel! Don't kill him! I love him!

MANUEL: Don't be silly. You're just saying that to keep him from being put up against the wall!

MARIFÉ: Then I want to die with him.

PORFIRIO (*Taking her in his arms.*): My sweetheart!

DON PEDRO (*Alarmed.*): Wait a minute. Wait a minute. This must be some kind of a joke. Isn't it?

Manuel motions for him to be quiet.

PORFIRIO: I had been waiting for you so long . . .

MARIFÉ: And I was going toward you with closed eyes . . .

PORFIRIO: My sunshine, my morning dew . . .

MANUEL: That's enough. I can leave now. Matters of state demand my attention!

PORFIRIO: I'm ready. But why can't you spare her?

MANUEL: Forget it, will you. It was Juanita's idea. The farce is over!

MARIFÉ: How cynical.

PORFIRIO (*Taken aback.*): Juanita's idea?

MANUEL: Well, you were sad! You carried your melancholy around with you through all the corridors of the palace! You were no longer good for anything! You were turning government duties over to Félix who is completely crazy! . . . I decided to become your successor! By acting out the farce of having you condemned to death, I succeeded in getting that lovely girl to admit she loves you. And there you are cured!

PORFIRIO (*Surprised.*): But explain to me how you took my place! I mean with whose support?

MANUEL: Simple! I proposed selling the second floor of the presidential palace to the Deutsch Bananian Company to be used also as a banana warehouse!

PORFIRIO (*Shocked.*): You did that? . . .

MANUEL: Well, you were the one who started it! . . .

DON PEDRO: How much are you going to get out of it?

MANUEL: The State will make 200,000 pesos!

DON PEDRO (*To Porfirio.*): See? I told you you could have asked twice as much!

PORFIRIO: You poor fool! . . . Where will the seat of government be after this?

MANUEL: In the attic! None of the banana companies wanted it! It's too hot up there!

A commotion is heard outside. Juanita appears like a madwoman.

SCENE 12

The same, plus Juanita.

JUANITA: Darling! There's been treason!

MANUEL: Get hold of yourself! What's going on sweetheart?

JUANITA (*Out of breath.*): General Félix has revolted during your absence!

DON PEDRO: Well, I'll be! . . . Manuel has beaten General Patitas's record!

MANUEL: Now I won't have the right to have a street named after me?

JUANITA: The thing is General Félix wants to arrest you.

PORFIRIO (*Flaring up.*): With him you never know . . . To arms!

MANUEL: Careful. Someone's coming. Watch out on port side!

SCENE 13

The same, plus Doña Cumacha.

DON PEDRO: Doña Cumacha!

DOÑA CUMACHA: Ah! You're all here! . . . If you only knew . . . How dreadful!

DON PEDRO: Now my sweet. Get a grip on yourself . . . What's going on?

DOÑA CUMACHA (*Faltering.*): Horrible! Horrible! Horrible!

DON PEDRO (*Alarmed.*): There must be shocking scenes of debauchery going on in the square.

DOÑA CUMACHA (*Same as before.*): Hideous! Hideous! Hideous!

PORFIRIO: What then?

DOÑA CUMACHA (*Calming down.*): Do you know how Félix was able to seize power?

PORFIRIO: Tell me quick!

DOÑA CUMACHA: He sold the crypt of the Pantheon to the Anglo Banana Company!

PORFIRIO: Damn it! Sacrilege! Desecration!

MANUEL: The Pantheon's crypt . . . where all our national glories are enshrined!

DOÑA CUMACHA: Since its vaults are cool, it will be used to store bananas.

PORFIRIO: That's too much! Let's revolt. To arms! We will give this vile traitor no quarter!

MANUEL: He's right!

MARIFÉ, JUANITA, DOÑA CUMACHA (*Together.*): Wait a little while. Calm down.

PORFIRIO: No, no. Death to the traitor!

Manuel and his sailors also shout for death while marching around in a circle. Doña Cumacha throws her arms in the air and Don Pedro goes to replace Manuel's portrait by one of General Félix.

DON PEDRO (*Winking at the public.*): You never know!

Outside the public is acclaiming Félix. Bombita, for his part, is shouting hysterically: "Long live liberty! Long live Félix! . . . One banana! Two bananas! Three bananas! Four bananas!" Suddenly a stupendous explosion is heard outside. Shouts of horror. Panic, Women shriek in the darkness. When the light comes back on, Gamello appears, his face black with powder, his clothing shredded. He's beaming with joy, however, and shouting.

GAMELLO: It went off! Right under Félix's behind! He didn't have faith in it. He threw it down. Boom! It exploded under him right in the middle of the Pantheon! All his file cards in the air! Boom! It exploded!

He takes Doña Cumacha in his arms and leads her off while she protests and everyone shouts with joy. Finally, during the hubbub, down comes the

CURTAIN

Drawing by Jean Brune.—Courtesy of
Emmanuel Roblès

Juanita and Marifé fanning and trying to pacify their mother, Doña Cumacha (seated), who is upset because she fears her two daughters have been up to no good.—Photograph of the Théâtre de l'Essor production, Tunis, 1958, courtesy of Emmanuel Roblès

Scene from *Porfirio*.—Photograph of the Théâtre de l'Essor production, Tunis, 1958, courtesy of Emmanuel Roblès

Scene from an African production of *Porfirio*, performed in 1971 at Fort-Lamy, Republic of Chad.—Photograph courtesy of Emmanuel Roblès

Bibliography of the Theatre of Roblès

BY MARIE J. KILKER

The following original plays and theatrical adaptations by Roblès are arranged chronologically by order of writing.

Original Plays

"Ile Déserte." *Revue Périples*, No. 5 (Feb. 1948).
Ile Déserte/Desert Isle. Collection Réversible. St. Louis: Francité, 1975.
"Montserrat." *Le Monde illustré: Théâtral et Littéraire*, No. 26 (5 June 1948), 1–30.
Montserrat. Paris: Charlot, 1949; rpt. Paris: Seuil, 1954; avec 29 hors texte. Paris: Seuil, 1962.
Montserrat. Ed. illustrée et annotée à l'usage de l'enseignement. Antwerp: de Sikkel, 1965.
La Vérité est morte. Paris: Seuil, 1952.
L'Horloge suivi de Porfirio. Paris: Seuil, 1958; rev. ed., 1974.
"Porfirio, ou L'Age d'or." *Magazine de l'Afrique du Nord*, Nos. 25–27 (March, May, July 1952).
Porfirio. Algiers: Rivages, 1953.
"L'Etrange immeuble de la rue Marconi." *Simoun*, Nos. 6–7 (1953), 67–137. (Original of *L'Horloge*.)
Plaidoyer pour un rebelle suivi de Mer libre. Paris: Seuil, 1965.
Les Yaquils/Yaquils. With a workshop translation by Anne-Marie Hamburg. Collection Réversible. St. Louis: Theatre-in-Translation, 1972.
La Fenêtre. Unpublished, but performed and recorded by Radio Montreal. 1975.

Theatrical Adaptations

Cervantes, Miguel de. *Le vieux jaloux*. Collection Mediterranée vivante. Algiers: Rivages, 1950, 1954. (Original: *El Viejo Celoso*.)
———. *L'Espagnol courageux*. Oran: Les Cahiers de Santa Cruz, 1958; rpts. *Simoun*, Nos. 28–29 (1958), 33–113; *Les Oeuvres Libres*, No. 217 (June 1964), Arthème Fayard. (Original: *El Gallardo Español*.)
Mihura, Miguel. "Carlota." *Paris-Théâtre*, No. 161, pp. 10–46. Resumé: "Emmanuel Roblès raconte: *Carlota* de Miguel Mihura." *l'Avant Scène*, No. 218 (15 April 1960), 37–39. (Original: *A media luz tres*.)

————. "L'Ane bleu." Unpublished, but performed. 1960. (Original: *A media luz tres.*)

Hansberry, Lorraine. *Un Raisin au soleil.* Trans. Philippe Bonnière. Nouveaux Horizons. Paris: Seghers, 1963. (Original: *A Raisin in the Sun.*)

Nicolaj, Aldo. "Le Soldat piccico." Unpublished, not performed, but under contract to the Théâtre Royal du Parc, Brussels. 1968. (Original: *Il Soldato Piccico.*)

Works Devoted to Roblès

Astre, George-Albert. *Emmanuel Roblès ou l'homme et son espoir.* Paris: Périples, 1972.

d'Aubrac, Jacques, general ed. *Dossier Roblès.* Collection "Dossiers." Paris: J. T. F., 1965.

Depierris, Jean-Louis. *Entretiens avec Emmanuel Roblès.* Paris: Seuil, 1967.

Eliade, Bernard. *Lecture-animation de Montserrat.* Paris: Gamma, 1974.

Frigiotti, Josette. *Roblès Dramaturge: Essai de théâtre comparé.* Paris: Scènes de France, 1972.

Kilker, Marie J. Petrone. *The Theatre of Emmanuel Roblès: An American Introduction with a Checklist on Criticism and Production.* Diss. Southern Illinois University at Carbondale, 1972.

Landi-Bénos, Fanny. *Emmanuel Roblès ou Les raisons de vivre.* Avec une lettre-préface d'Emmanuel Roblès. Paris: P. J. Oswald, 1969.

Livres de France, 16, No. 2 (Feb. 1965); rpt. *Bibliographie,* 33, No. 2 (Feb. 1965).

"Pour saluer Roblès," *Simoun,* No. 30 (Dec. 1959).

Rozier, Micheline A. *Emmanuel Roblès ou la rupture du cercle.* Collection "Etudes." Sherbrooke, Qué.: Naaman, 1973.

Criticism of the Plays in Publication

Plaidoyer pour un rebelle

A., R. "*Plaidoyer pour un rebelle suivi de Mer libre.*" *Reflets du Luxembourg,* 5 July 1965.

Chwat, Paul. "Entretien avec Emmanuel Roblès, auteur de *Plaidoyer pour un rebelle,* et *Mer libre,* deux tragédies de notre temps." *Paris Europe Magazine,* No. 15 (13 June 1965), 1–4.

Leon, Georges. "*Le Plaidoyer:* Un homme à la fraternité." *Humanité,* 1 June 1965.

M., C. "Deux pièces à lire d'Emmanuel Roblès." *Carrefour,* 30 June 1965.

Ravussin, Charles. "Antigone pour aujourd'hui." *Le Journal de Ge-nève*, 17 Oct. 1965.
Review of *Plaidoyer pour un rebelle suivi de Mer libre. Bulletin critique du livre français*, 20, No. 6 (June 1965), 510–11.
Ribas, Joseph. "Emmanuel Roblès: 'Mon théâtre? Une crise et un por-trait.'" *Dépêche du Midi*, 15 June 1965.
"Rive gauche, rive droite: Du neuf dans la presse." *Gazette de Lausanne*: "La Gazette littéraire," 9–10 (Oct. 1965), 14.
Rousselot, Jean. "L'omelette et les oeufs." *Le Coopérateur*, 30 Oct. 1965.
———. "Roblès et le monde réel." *Les Lettres françaises*, 20 May 1965, pp. 1, 6.
Semet, Roger. "La Voie aux chapitres." *Le Canard enchaîné*, 9 June 1965.
Tournis, G. "Roblès: Théâtre II." *Inst. Pédag. National*, April 1967.

L'Horloge and *Porfirio*

Bensimon, Marc. "French Fiction: *L'Horloge. Porfirio.*" *Books Abroad*, 33, No. 1 (Winter 1959), 44.
Bergeron, Régis. "Abdallah le croquant." *Humanité*, 24 July 1958.
Bohr, Joey. "Le rôle de la femme dans quatre pièces d'Emmanuel Ro-blès." *Francité*, No. 1 (1972), 58–78.
C., J. "Les livres." *Cité nouvelle*, 16 June 1960.
Kröjer, Maxim. "Studies, Stukken en Tijdschriften." *Her Hand-elsblad*, 21 Aug. 1958.
Penz, Charles. "Dans la corbeille à ouvrages." *Marocaine Casablanca*, 4 Jan. 1959.
Roblès, Emmanuel. "Nous parle de *Porfirio.*" *Scènes de France*, No. 15 (March 1965), 9.
T. "Où la révolution des colonels en prend pour son grade." *Le Canard enchaîné*, 16 July 1958.
V., S. de. "Le théâtre d'Emmanuel Roblès." *La Libre Belgique*, 27 Aug. 1958.
Volmane, Véra. "Théâtre: *L'Horloge suivi de Porfirio.*" *Les Nouvelles littéraires*, 31 July 1958, p. 3.
Wurmser, André. "Les jeunes romanciers devant la guerre d'Algérie." *Les Lettres françaises*, 3 July 1958, pp. 1–2.

Reviews of the Plays in Performance

Plaidoyer pour un rebelle

Curtins, A. "Vordem Fernsehschirm." *Frankenpost*, 13 Dec. 1965.
Dannecker, Hermann. "Plädoyer für einen Rebellen." *Badische Neueste Nachrichten*, 3 April 1965.
"Fanatiker und Idealisten." *Kieler Nachrichten*, 11 Dec. 1965.
"Gutes *Plädoyer für einen Rebellen.*" *Sudkurier*, 13 Dec. 1965.

Hauck, Lore. "Viele Vorhänge für deutsche Erstaufführung." *Frankenpost*, 25 March 1965.

J[ansen]., A. "Un quart d'heure avec Emmanuel Roblès: ou le terrorism au théâtre." *Le Soir*, 14 April 1966.

L., J. "Les Spectacles à Bruxelles: Théâtre engagé au Théâtre du Parc." *La Cité*, 15 April 1966.

Ledent, Roger. "Au Parc: une pièce fort bien mise en scène." *La Lanterne*, 15 April 1966.

Ledoux, Clément. "Sang et eau." *Le Canard enchaîné*, 25 Aug. 1966.

Paris, André. "*Plaidoyer pour un rebelle*: L'indépendance ne peut-elle jamais s'acheter qu'au prix du sang?" *Le Soir*, 14 April 1966.

Paul, Wolfgang. "Kolonialdrama." *Der Tagesspiegel*, 11 Dec. 1965.

"Rebell in Indonesien." *Münchner Merkur*, 11 Dec. 1965.

Riemens, Leo. "Een Toneelstuk Vol Sfeer En Visuelle Vondsten." *De Telegraaf*, 19 Jan. 1968.

"Une création 'brûlante' au Parc." *Soir Illustré*, 7 April 1966.

L'Horloge

Crew, Louie. "Prominent Theatrical People Attend *The Clock* Performance." *Orangeburg Times and Democrat*, 7 Dec. 1972, p. 3-C.

Meslin, Jean. "*L'Horloge* sonne pour la Compagnie des Deux Rives l'heure de se hisser à l'échelle du succès." *La Nouvelle République*, 15 Jan. 1965.

Porfirio

Bertrand, Joseph. "Les critiques de la semaine." *Les Beaux-Arts*, 20 May 1960.

Chesselet, Robert. "*Porfirio* ou l'histoire d'une révolution rigolote." *La Lanterne*, 5 May 1960.

"Heureuse association: Roblès–Ravez." *Dimanche-Presse*, 8 May 1960.

"Le premier spectacle de l'Essor pour la saison a triomphé avec *Porfirio*." *Dépêche Tunisienne*, 19 Nov. 1958.

S., R. "Avec Emmanuel Roblès, Jacques Vingler et la Comédie de Besançon, on a éclaté de rire sous *Porfirio*." *L'Est Républicain*, 12 March 1965.

Smal, Christian-Guy. "Une création au théâtre de Quat' Sous." *Le Peuple*, 5 May 1960.

"Un spectacle de classe." *La Presse*, 18 Nov. 1958.